ANCIENT GREEK ART AND ARCHITECTURE

by Don Nardo

LUCENT BOOKS
A part of Gale, Cengage Learning

Detroit • New York • San Francisco • New Haven, Conn • Waterville, Maine • London

© 2012 Gale, Cengage Learning

LIBRARY OF CONGRESS CATALOGING-IN-PUBLICATION DATA

Nardo, Don, 1947-
 Ancient Greek art and architecture / by Don Nardo.
  p. cm. -- (Eye on art)
 Includes bibliographical references and index.
 ISBN 978-1-4205-0685-3 (hardcover)
 1. Art, Greek--Juvenile literature. 2. Architecture, Greek--Juvenile
literature. I. Title.
 N5630.N37 2011
 709.38--dc23
                                                            2011028048

Lucent Books
27500 Drake Rd
Farmington Hills MI 48331

ISBN-13: 978-1-4205-0685-3
ISBN-10: 1-4205-0685-4

Printed in the United States of America
1 2 3 4 5 6 7 15 14 13 12 11

Contents

Foreword

"Art has no other purpose than to brush aside . . . everything that veils reality from us in order to bring us face to face with reality itself."

—French philosopher Henri-Louis Bergson

Some thirty-one thousand years ago, early humans painted strikingly sophisticated images of horses, bison, rhinoceroses, bears, and other animals on the walls of a cave in southern France. The meaning of these elaborate pictures is unknown, although some experts speculate that they held ceremonial significance. Regardless of their intended purpose, the Chauvet-Pont-d'Arc cave paintings represent some of the first known expressions of the artistic impulse.

From the Paleolithic era to the present day, human beings have continued to create works of visual art. Artists have developed painting, drawing, sculpture, engraving, and many other techniques to produce visual representations of landscapes, the human form, religious and historical events, and countless other subjects. The artistic impulse also finds expression in glass, jewelry, and new forms inspired by new technology. Indeed, judging by humanity's prolific artistic output throughout history, one must conclude that the compulsion to produce art is an inherent aspect of being human, and the results are among humanity's greatest cultural achievements: masterpieces such as the architectural marvels of ancient Greece, Michelangelo's perfectly rendered statue *David*, Vincent van Gogh's visionary painting *Starry Night*, and endless other treasures.

The creative impulse serves many purposes for society. At its most basic level, art is a form of entertainment or the means for a satisfying or pleasant aesthetic experience. But art's true power lies not in its potential to entertain and delight but in its ability to enlighten, to reveal the truth, and by doing so to uplift the human spirit and transform the human race.

One of the primary functions of art has been to serve religion. For most of Western history, for example, artists were paid by the church to produce works with religious themes and subjects. Art was thus a tool to help human beings transcend mundane, secular reality and achieve spiritual enlightenment. One of the best-known, and largest-scale, examples of Christian religious art is the Sistine Chapel in the Vatican in Rome. In 1508 Pope Julius II commissioned Italian Renaissance artist Michelangelo to paint the chapel's vaulted ceiling, an area of 640 square yards (535 sq. m). Michelangelo spent four years on scaffolding, his neck craned, creating a panoramic fresco of some three hundred human figures. His paintings depict Old Testament prophets and heroes, sibyls of Greek mythology, and nine scenes from the Book of Genesis, including the Creation of Adam, the Fall of Adam and Eve from the Garden of Eden, and the Flood. The ceiling of the Sistine Chapel is considered one of the greatest works of Western art and has inspired the awe of countless Christian pilgrims and other religious seekers. As eighteenth-century German poet and author Johann Wolfgang von Goethe wrote, "Until you have seen this Sistine Chapel, you can have no adequate conception of what man is capable of."

In addition to inspiring religious fervor, art can serve as a force for social change. Artists are among the visionaries of any culture. As such, they often perceive injustice and wrongdoing and confront others by reflecting what they see in their work. One classic example of art as social commentary was created in May 1937, during the brutal Spanish civil war. On May 1 Spanish artist Pablo Picasso learned of the recent attack on the small Basque village of Guernica by German airplanes allied with fascist forces led by Francisco Franco. The German pilots had used the village for target practice, a three-hour bombing that killed sixteen hundred civilians. Picasso, living in Paris, channeled his outrage over the massacre into his painting *Guernica,* a black, white, and gray mural that depicts dismembered animals and fractured human figures whose faces are contorted in agonized expressions. Initially, critics and the public condemned the painting as an incoherent hodgepodge, but the work soon came to be seen as a powerful antiwar statement and remains an iconic symbol of the violence and terror that dominated world events during the remainder of the twentieth century.

The impulse to create art—whether painting animals with crude pigments on a cave wall, sculpting a human form from marble, or commemorating human tragedy in a mural—thus serves many purposes. It offers an entertaining diversion, nourishes the imagination and the spirit, decorates and beautifies the world, and chronicles the age. But underlying all these functions is the desire to reveal that which is obscure—to illuminate, clarify, and perhaps ennoble. As Picasso himself stated, "The purpose of art is washing the dust of daily life off our souls."

The Eye on Art series is intended to assist readers in understanding the various roles of art in society. Each volume offers an in-depth exploration of a major artistic movement, medium, figure, or profession. All books in the series are beautifully illustrated with full-color photographs and diagrams. Riveting narrative, clear technical explanation, informative sidebars, fully documented quotes, a bibliography, and a thorough index all provide excellent starting points for research and discussion. With these features, the Eye on Art series is a useful introduction to the world of art—a world that can offer both insight and inspiration.

Introduction

The First Westerners

Nearly every past civilization had its artists—sometimes painters, sculptors, architects, master potters, goldsmiths, or at times all of these and more. Moreover, it is likely that each of these cultures could claim a few artistic geniuses of the caliber of Raphael (the great Italian Renaissance painter) or Frank Lloyd Wright (the brilliant early twentieth-century American architect). Yet no peoples, past or present, have been as inherently artistic at their core and as successful in their artistic output as the ancient Greeks. In the words of the late art historian and critic Thomas Craven, considering

> their major glories in architecture and sculpture, their temples and their carved figures, [along with] the most beautiful necklaces ever to adorn a woman's throat . . . they remain the most artistic race in the history of human-kind. . . . Man for man, carving for carving, and temple for temple, there was more art in the soul of the average Greek than has ever been centered in the soul of the average good citizen of any commonwealth anywhere.[1]

To Stand the Tests of Time

Exactly why the Greeks had such an artistic spirit, such a love of art, and such an eagerness to create art remains uncertain.

Certainly various historians and other experts have tried to explain it. One whose attempt was especially notable was the great classical scholar Edith Hamilton. Before her death in 1963, she remarked that with the Greeks,

The Greeks' celebration of life distinguished the ancient Greek spirit from that of their contemporaries.

> something completely new came into the world. They were the first Westerners [European-based peoples]. The spirit of the West, the modern spirit, is a Greek discovery, and the place of the Greeks is in the modern world. . . . Somewhere among those steep stone mountains, in little sheltered valleys where the great hills were ramparts [battlements] to defend and men could have security for peace and happy living . . . the joy of life found expression. [To] rejoice in life, to find the world beautiful and delightful to live in was a mark of

the Greek spirit which distinguished it from all that had gone before. It is a vital distinction. The joy of life is written upon everything the Greeks left behind, and [this is] something that is of first importance in understanding how the Greek achievement came to pass.[2]

Another noted scholar of ancient Greece, the late C.M. Bowra, speculated differently about why the Greeks produced such a large and magnificent body of art, particularly architecture, sculpture, ceramics (pottery), and painting. First, he said, Greek artists did not create things wholesale, for a large, anonymous public, as so many artists do today. Instead, they worked for specific patrons (including sometimes the state, or government), who hired them to produce items for specific and often special reasons. When the state hired a sculptor, for example, his work "was meant to be seen in public places, principally in temples," Bowra pointed out. "And it had to be worthy of the gods. It had to have nobility and dignity."[3] Thus, work of the highest possible quality was expected of artists, and most of them delivered just that.

Also, Bowra wrote, the Greeks—artists, writers, and political leaders alike—were very preoccupied with their images. They worried not only about what other Greeks and foreigners thought of them, but also about what their descendants might think. "The Greeks wanted their arts and handicrafts to stand the acid tests of time and to keep their attractions for future generations. In this fashion, they hoped to prolong their own influence into the future."[4]

To the Victors, the Spoils

It must be emphasized that the Greeks to whom Craven, Hamilton, and Bowra mainly refer were those who lived when Greek civilization was more or less at its height. They are most often called the classical Greeks. Strictly speaking, Greece's Classical Age, as determined by modern experts, lasted from about 500 to 323 B.C. The period that preceded it is called the Archaic Age (circa 800–500 B.C.), and scholars call the era that followed the Classical Age the Hellenistic Age (323–c. 30 B.C.) As a sort of historical shorthand, however, the term *classical Greeks* is often used in a general way to describe the Greeks from about 750 to 300 B.C.

The bulk of the great sculptures, structures, and other examples of art the Greeks produced were made during the Classical and Hellenistic periods. In the Archaic Age, by contrast, Greek artists were still learning and experimenting with various materials, tools, and methods. After the Hellenistic Age, artists still thrived in the Greek lands, but by that time those lands were under Roman rule. The Romans did commission some artworks from the Greeks. But more often Roman generals looted statues and other artistic items from Greek cities and brought them to Roman Italy. The sad fact, scholar Nigel Spivey says, is that there was "a generally recognized rule in antiquity [ancient times] that precious cultural possessions were liable to seizure by the victors. So [in] ancient Greece, [much accumulated art became] the spoils and booty of war. . . . Greek art suffered badly [as powerful] Romans abused their power in amassing private collections of Greek statues and other artworks."[5]

Put simply, when the Greeks became a conquered people, their tradition of producing great, original art waned. Sculptors were hired to carve knockoffs of earlier classic statues, for instance, and in time some artists were making knockoffs of knockoffs. Whatever masterpieces they may have created from time to time were Roman property, further robbing the Greeks of their pride in accomplishment.

The Greco-Roman Fusion

Fortunately for posterity, however, Rome's absorption of Greece, including its arts, proved to be a good thing. Despite their many talents and strengths, which allowed them to gain dominance over the Mediterranean world, the Romans readily recognized the superiority of Greek culture. So they copied and absorbed it at every turn. They steadily incorporated Greek religious ideas, literature, philosophy, and artistic

A Roman copy of the Greek sculpture of Apollo as a lyre player. The Romans incorporated Greek religious ideas, literature, philosophy, and artistic styles and techniques into their culture and spread them throughout the Mediterranean world.

styles and techniques, in the process transforming their own, less sophisticated culture. In a very real way, the Greeks made the Romans Westerners, too. The result was the Greco-Roman cultural fusion that eventually came to be called "classical" civilization.

More importantly, when the western Roman Empire disintegrated in the fifth and sixth centuries A.D., medieval Europe inherited numerous aspects of classical culture, including some Greek ones. In the fullness of time, these passed along to the modern world. Thus, even though they conquered Greece, the Romans kept the Greek arts alive. They helped make it possible for the splendid remnants of Greece's immense artistic achievement to gain immortality and for people today to marvel at it. In the long list of Rome's own noteworthy achievements, this may well have been the greatest.

1

The Art of Greece's Bronze Age

In early modern times classical Greek art, especially architecture and sculpture, became standards of excellence against which all other artistic styles and forms were measured or compared. Across the Western world, agents from museums and private collectors alike scoured Greece's many ruined sites. They bought, and sometimes outright stole, whatever artistic remnants they could find and brought them back to their home countries. There, cultural prestige was often measured in part by how many authentic ancient artworks one owned and displayed, and Greek art was the most esteemed of all. Meanwhile, no books or articles about art history were complete without thorough examinations of classical Greek artworks.

All of this collecting, displaying, appreciating, and status building associated with Greek art illustrates one major advantage modern civilization has over that of the classical Greeks. People today have developed a well-formed understanding of where they came from. They rely on archaeology and other kinds of science to describe the various past civilizations and explain how each fits into a sort of historical and cultural family tree. The ancient Greeks, with their magnificent artistic tradition, occupy a major branch of that tree, one that leads directly to contemporary Western culture.

In contrast, the Greeks themselves did not have a clear picture of where they or their artistic traditions came from. They relied instead on myths to describe the past. Some of these tales were completely fabricated, while others were distorted memories of real bygone people and events. Creation myths told how the world came to be and how the gods created humans from clay. There were also stories about the origins of the art forms the classical Greeks utilized. Like other creation myths, these held that someone in the dim past had to have created them more or less out of nothing.

STATUES THAT COULD SEE AND WALK

The classical Greeks had no credible idea how old their art traditions were. So they turned to myths about ancient artists, including ancient fables about Daedalus, said to have lived in the so-called Age of Heroes (the late Greek Bronze Age). He supposedly produced Greece's first sculptural and architectural works. The first-century-B.C. Greek historian Diodorus Siculus described some of Daedalus's accomplishments, saying:

Daedalus was an Athenian by birth, [and] surpassing all others in natural ability, he pursued with zeal the art of building and also of fashioning statues and carving stone. He was the discoverer of many devices that contributed to the development of art, and he produced marvelous works in many parts of the inhabited world. In the production of statues, he so excelled all other men that later generations preserved a story to the effect that the statues he created were exactly like living beings, for they say that they could see, and walk, and . . . the statue produced by art seemed to be a living being. . . . [Daedalus] was marveled at, quite naturally, by other men.

Diodorus Siculus. *Library of History*. Quoted in J.J. Pollitt, ed. and trans. *The Art of Ancient Greece: Sources and Documents*. New York: Cambridge University Press, 1990, p. 13.

Perhaps the most prominent of these legends claimed that a very ancient race, called the Telchines (tel-KY-neez), invented most of the arts. The Telchines supposedly dwelled on the large Aegean islands of Crete and Rhodes. The first-century-B.C. Greek historian Diodorus Siculus wrote: "They were the inventors of some of the arts and the introducers of other things that were useful for the life of men. [They] were also wizards and could summon clouds, storms, and hail whenever they wished. . . . It is also said that they could change their own shapes, and that they were jealous about giving instruction in their arts."⁶

Cycladic Art

The Telchines were clearly made up, or mythical people. Yet modern scholars think they constituted faint echoes of real artists or other people who lived in the Greek sphere many centuries before the classical Greeks arose. Archaeologists have shown that the first culturally advanced peoples to inhabit that sphere did in fact live on Crete and other southern Aegean Islands.

The earliest verified people in that region who produced what the modern world would identify as art belonged to what archaeologists call the Cycladic (ki-KLAD-ik or si-KLAD-ik) civilization. It is named for the main group of islands in the southern Aegean—the Cyclades. The known Cycladic occupation sites on these islands date from about 3300 to 2000 B.C. This roughly coincides with Greece's early Bronze Age, the period when people used tools and weapons made of bronze, an alloy of copper and tin.

The chief Cycladic art form discovered to date consists of carved marble figures, most of them nude females with their arms folded across the stomach. Modern experts assume these statues were meant to represent a nature goddess. Perhaps, they say, she was the most powerful deity worshipped in Cycladic society, although this has yet to be confirmed. One striking feature of these female figures is their form, or style. It is very abstract and lacking in realism or detail, much like similar carved figures in modern art. That style is a far cry from the stunningly lifelike sculptures the classical Greeks later produced.

Marble figurines from the Cycladic period, c. 2800–2300 B.C. The Cycladic peoples were the earliest producers of Greek art.

The Minoan Artistic Spirit

A considerably more culturally and artistically advanced Bronze Age Aegean people came to light in 1900. In that year British archaeologist Arthur Evans began to unearth the remains of an immense palace at Knossos (NOS-us, also spelled Knossus or Cnossus), near Crete's northern coast. It became clear to Evans that that island had been the central focus of a splendid civilization that had reached its height in about 1600 B.C. He dubbed the people the Minoans, after King Minos, a mythical Cretan ruler. Since that time, several more Minoan palaces, along with houses, pottery, paintings, and other artifacts, have been found. All reveal that the Minoans were the first advanced society not only in Greece, but in all of Europe. They were highly economically prosperous thanks to the vigorous trade they carried on with neighboring regions as far away as Egypt.

The Minoans also produced several forms of lively, often beautiful art. They initially borrowed many of their artistic fashions and techniques from the older cultures of the Middle East, particularly Egypt. Yet they did not merely copy these styles. Instead, they borrowed them, reorganized them, and applied them in new ways. As noted historian Sarah B. Pomeroy puts it:

> The spirit of Minoan art and architecture [was] very different [from that of the ancient Middle East]. The predominant function of palace art in the East was to glorify the royal household. The kings were depicted as mighty conquerors and powerful rulers. In Minoan art, on the other hand, there are no scenes that show the king as a conquering warrior and indeed very few, if any, images of royal pomp. The subjects and motifs [themes] of the wall paintings are [mainly about nature and everyday life]. The spirit of Minoan palace art is serene and happy, even playful at times. It is meant to make the palace a place of beauty and charm.[7]

Minoan art also featured a strong religious undercurrent. Although the paintings often show casual scenes from everyday life, they exhibit spiritual aspects as well. Because this element of their art is very subtle to the modern eye, it would not be very evident to most people today, but it would have been perfectly obvious to the average Minoan. Also, he or she did not view paintings and other art simply as a form of decoration. Rather, it expressed society's views of community standards and accepted social traditions. Indeed, a wall painting, in the words of one expert, "was a representation of the collective values of the society of which the viewer was a member. Thus, the relationship between art and the viewer was intimate and the function of the painting important."[8]

The Minoans produced several forms of lively, beautiful art, such as this fresco found at the palace-center at Knossos, in Crete.

Monumental Minoan Architecture

As they did in their small-scale arts, such as painting, the Minoans infused the art of monumental (large-scale) architecture with religious, social, and other dimensions. The palace-centers at Knossos and other Cretan sites are the chief surviving examples. According to the late historian Chester G. Starr, these unique structures

> consist of mazes of rooms and living quarters organized around central courtyards and well equipped with drains and baths. In their sprawling nature, they may well have been remembered in the later Greek myth of the "labyrinth" [in which dwelled a monster half-man and half-bull]. . . . The staircases and other architectural details of these buildings display on an intimate scale an aesthetic [artistic] sense which one may look for in vain in most Egyptian architecture.[9]

Starr's use of the word *maze* highlights one major aspect of Minoan architecture that made it different from that of Egypt and other parts of the Middle East. Namely, the Cretan palace-centers were very complex buildings featuring rambling, often multistoried and split-level clusters of corridors and chambers. Shapewise, some experts have compared such a structure to dozens of cardboard boxes of varying sizes piled into a haphazard, asymmetrical mass.

Within that great mass were literally hundreds of rooms and other architectural spaces surrounding a large, more or less central, courtyard. These included a throne room, royal apartments, broad staircases and stairwells, religious shrines, kitchens, bathrooms, workrooms, and all manner of storerooms. Light wells and small, open courtyards were ingeniously installed at intervals throughout the structure so that at least some sunlight reached all areas.

Particularly striking were the sophisticated plumbing facilities in the bathrooms. Using pipes made of baked clay, they provided running water and efficient waste removal. One researcher explains:

> There were even toilets, evidence of which is preserved in traces of seats over large drains that lead outside the palace. Wastes were flushed away by pouring water down an elaborate system of drains that included clay pipes carefully fitted together in sections and stone troughs to carry off rain water. The bathtubs, however, did not connect with the pipes. . . . Plugless, they apparently were bailed or sponged out by a servant when the bather was through washing, [and] the dirty water [was] thrown down the nearest drain.[10]

Archaeologists have demonstrated another important aspect of these grand structures. The workrooms and storerooms were used by dozens and in some cases hundreds of people as part of the local economy, which was based on agriculture and raising livestock. Also, community worship, rather than the

A reconstruction of the Minoan palace-center of Knossos. The Minoans infused the art of large scale architecture with religious and social dimensions.

THE MINOANS' DISTINCTIVE COLUMNS

A number of architectural features made Minoan palace-centers distinct from the palaces and other monumental buildings of other ancient cultures, both in the second millennium B.C. and in later ages. One was the shape and color of the columns that supported the upper floors of the palace-centers. Unlike Greek and Roman columns, for example, which were the same width at the bottom and top, Minoan columns significantly tapered downward. Also, the Minoans painted their columns black and bright red. One of the biographers of Arthur Evans, who excavated the first Minoan palace-center found in modern times, writes:

T he most likely explanation for the downward taper was that the tree trunks used in ancient times were unseasoned and the best way to keep unseasoned timber from sprouting was to plant it upside-down. The Minoans had painted their graceful columns either red or black, with the capitals [tops] made wide enough to throw rainwater clear of the base, which might otherwise rot.

Sylvia L. Horwitz. *The Find of a Lifetime: Sir Arthur Evans and the Discovery of Knossos.* London: Phoenix, 2001, pp. 139–140.

The distinctive tapered columns, characteristic of Minoan style, are shown in the palace-center of Knossos in Crete.

private rituals of the leaders alone, took place in the massive central courtyard. Thus, such buildings were not merely royal residences. They were also administrative, economic, and religious centers as well. This is why scholars came to call them "palace-centers" rather than simply "palaces."

Minoan Painting

Evidence shows that the Minoan palace-centers were filled with wall paintings of various sizes, as were smaller private houses. One such residence, which excavators dubbed the "House of the Frescos" (located northwest of the Knossos palace-center), contains several stunning frescoes. In the fresco technique, the artist first applies a coating of plaster to a wall or other surface. Then he or she applies paint directly onto the wet plaster, so that the two substances merge and dry together.

The styles and themes of Minoan painting are as distinctive as the monumental architecture of that culture. Noted archaeologist William R. Biers remarks:

> In Minoan paintings, spontaneity and love of life are expressed in bright colors. They are naturalistic, but the artist was not afraid of changing colors or distorting natural shapes in order to convey feeling or emotion. Many of the frescoes exhibit a quick, sketchy technique that forced the artist to concentrate on the particular parts of the picture that were most important to him. . . . Paintings found in Crete vary in size from life-sized figures to miniature frescoes in which the figures are quite small. Floors may also have been painted.[11]

Of the two main categories of subject matter in the Minoan paintings, the first consists of scenes from nature. An outstanding example is the Flying Fish fresco, found in a Minoan-period site on the Aegean island of Melos. It features winged fish, colored blue, yellow, and white, that seem to zoom through strings of seaweed, giving a remarkably realistic sensation of rapid, chaotic motion.

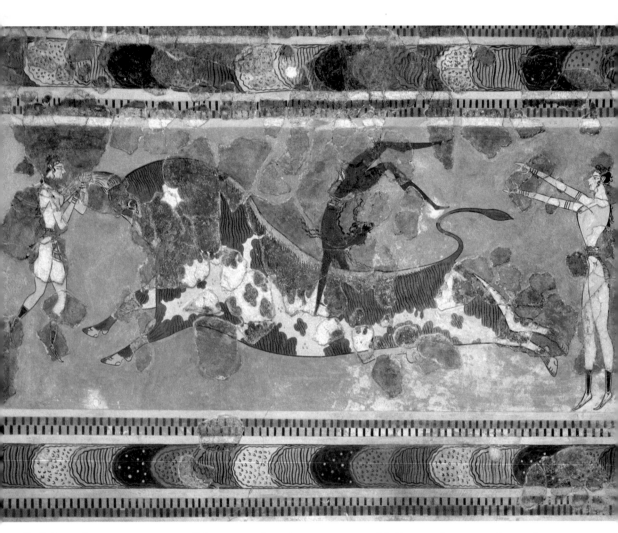

Bull-jumping frescoes have been found at Knossos and elsewhere. They depict athletic men and woman leaping over the backs of giant bulls.

The second major category of Minoan frescoes shows images of men and women engaged in various activities, mostly related to the royal court, religious worship, and public celebrations. Arthur Evans himself described a fresco he found that shows crowds of people gathered for a public festivity: "We recognize court ladies in elaborate [attire]. [They] are seated in groups with their legs half bent under them, engaged in animated conversation emphasized by expressive gesticulation [hand-gestures]. . . . The men, none of whom are bearded, are naked except for [a] loincloth and footgear."[12]

Also famous in this category of Minoan art are the bull-jumping frescoes found at Knossos and elsewhere. They depict athletic-looking young men and women leaping over the backs of giant bulls. (Bulls were sacred animals in Minoan religion.)

Ceramics and Other Crafts

Minoan artisans created other artworks and fine crafts besides wall paintings. In their earliest period, before the rise of the sophisticated palace-centers, their pottery was made either without potter's wheels or with very basic ones that turned slowly. Also, these items were baked in ordinary wood fires. Later, in the more advanced society that produced the palace-centers, a faster potter's wheel was developed. Also, stone kilns, which allowed potters more control over the firing process, came into use, permitting them to turn out items of higher quality. These items included pitchers, teapots, cups, bowls, goblets, frying pans, strainers, large and small storage jars, and numerous others. They were most often decorated with repeating patterns of images from nature, including flowers, leaves, grasses, sea plants, and sea creatures. Especially popular were octopi with long, flowing tentacles, a frequent image in Minoan art.

These ceramic products are not only fine examples of ancient art, but also extremely valuable to modern scholars. This is because they underwent small, steady changes in style and technique over time, and each new stylistic phase was distinct from the ones that preceded and followed it. As a result, today's experts can roughly date the various stages of Minoan (and later Greek) civilization by examining the remnants of pottery objects found at various excavation sites.

Among other examples of Minoan arts and crafts are jars, vases, bowls and other items made of carved stone, metal, bone, shell, and ivory. The stone objects were probably inspired by the Egyptians, who excelled in the production of stoneware. But Minoan artisans became no less expert at this craft, turning out objects carved from gypsum, obsidian, serpentine, alabaster, limestone, and marble. In the meantime, Minoan metalworkers utilized copper, bronze, gold, and silver. The copper and bronze items included eating utensils, cooking pots, swords, and armor, among many others. Gold and silver were used to make not only exquisite drinking cups for the wealthy, but also jewelry and decorative inlays for wooden storage chests.

Wooden chests and other kinds of furniture found at Knossos and other Cretan sites are also inlaid with shell and ivory. Ivory was used to fashion game boards and playing pieces as well. A splendidly crafted game board discovered in the ruins of Knossos features small amounts of gold, silver, and crystal mixed with the ivory. Minoan figurines contained ivory, too, including the so-called Boston Goddess (also known as Snake Goddess), a statuette of a female deity holding snakes, also unearthed at Knossos.

Mainland Architecture

In the same era in which Minoan civilization was thriving on Crete and other islands, another people, who spoke an early form of Greek, dwelled on the Greek mainland. Modern scholars call them the Mycenaeans (my-si-NEE-uns), named after one of their chief strongholds—Mycenae (my-SEE-nee), in southeastern Greece. The mainlanders' art, along with their culture in general, was long strongly influenced by the Minoans. "In a sense," Biers, writes, "Minoan-Mycenaean art is a unit, particularly where religious scenes are concerned." However, Mycenaean art was by no means identical to its Minoan counterpart. As Biers points out, the mainland version "has a distinctive flavor of its own, to be seen in some choices of subject matter . . . in the formalism of its designs, which are progressively more abstract versions of motifs inherited from the Minoans; and in large-scale sculpture."[13]

Such differences can be readily seen in the Mycenaeans' monumental architecture. Like the Minoans, they erected large palaces. But these were a bit smaller than the Minoan versions, as well as considerably more fortress-like, so experts sometimes refer to them as palace-citadels or just citadels. Their walls were made from enormous, roughly trimmed boulders, some of them 10 to 20 feet (3m to 6m) or more thick. They were so large that when the Greeks who lived there centuries later saw the ruins of these structures, they thought they had been constructed by the Cyclopes (sy-KLOH-peez), a legendary race of one-eyed giants.

The outer perimeter of the compound at Mycenae (in which the royal palace was only one of several buildings) exhibits these so-called Cyclopean (sy-kluh-PEE-un) walls. Of particular note is the renowned Lion Gate, which was apparently the main entrance to the compound. More than 10 feet (3m) high, the portal is topped by a massive sculpture of two lions guarding a sacred pillar, an image that may have been prominent in Mycenaean royal and/or religious art. Those stone lions are among only a handful of Mycenaean sculptures that have survived. But archaeologists believe that many more existed when the civilization was at its height in the late Bronze Age.

The Lion Gate at Mycenae shows two lions guarding a sacred pillar. It is among the few Mycenaean sculptures to have survived.

The rooms of the Mycenaean palace-citadels were grouped around a large central hall called a *megaron*. Nigel Spivey calls it

> a galleried hall whose central feature was a hearth. It was approached by a prominent porch and might include an antechamber [large foyer], too. Around flanking corridors, many smaller rooms might cluster. But the megaron—literally "large room," or "hall"—was, with its central fireplace, the focal point of palace life. The recovery of thrones in such rooms encourages the theory that this is where Mycenaean royalty conducted its business.[14]

As formidable as these mainland fortresses were, they were unable to protect their builders indefinitely. In about 1200 B.C., the Mycenaeans, who had two centuries before conquered Crete and the other Minoan sites, were themselves overwhelmed by waves of attackers. (The attackers' identity is still debated, but they probably came from southeastern Europe.) The Greek sphere, along with large portions of the Middle East, suffered drastic upheaval, and Greece's Bronze Age civilization suddenly went into irreversible decline. Greece entered a dark age in which literacy, record keeping, and artistic skills and production were mostly lost. The ruined palaces on Crete and the mainland and the powerful folk who ruled them faded into folklore, tales that slowly but steadily became part of the mythology of a new race of Greeks. When the Greeks emerged from the long dark age, they created an awesome body of art that would inspire the world ever after.

Monumental Architecture: Temples

Greece's Dark Age, set in motion by the collapse of its Bronze Age society, lasted from about 1100 to 800 B.C. It was characterized by the loss of literacy, population decreases, extensive poverty, and a major lapse in the production of monumental architecture, sculpture, and other arts. Meanwhile, as the Minoan-Mycenaean world gradually passed into legend, the surviving Greeks more or less forgot their heritage. As time went on, they recalled only bits and pieces of the past that crystallized into an elaborate mythology. Filled with heroes, monsters, and gods interacting with humans, its tales glamorized the dimly remembered prior era, which the Greeks came to call the Age of Heroes. For later Greeks, Chester G. Starr points out, the myths describing that age became "a fertile source of ideas for dramatists, philosophers, and artists."[15]

Due to widespread poverty that discouraged and largely prevented the production of artworks, those artists were unable to express themselves in major ways until Greece finally recovered from the Dark Age. Throughout the eighth century B.C.—the first portion of the Archaic Age (circa 800–500 B.C.)—towns grew in size and population. Also, the volume of trade among

This reconstruction of ancient Sparta is fanciful and exaggerated. The Spartans spent most of their money on their army and devoted relatively few funds to the kind of monumental architecture pictured here.

them and with neighboring regions increased. As a result, local economies within the Greek sphere expanded, and there was once again sufficient money and motivation to support the arts.

Also during Archaic times, the larger towns developed into examples of a new sociopolitical unit—the city-state. A typical Greek city-state consisted of a central town, or urban center, often built around a central hill (acropolis), which was fortified in case of attack. Clustered around the urban center were small villages and farms, whose crops and livestock supported the whole community. Each city-state saw itself as a tiny, separate nation and fiercely guarded its borders and local traditions. Those traditions included artistic ones.

The Most Visible Art

During Greece's Archaic Age and the Classical Age (circa 500–323 B.C.) that followed it, certain architectural, sculptural, and other styles of art became common to all Greeks. However, each major city-state developed distinctive variations of its own. Also, some states concentrated more of their financial resources and energies on the arts than others.

Sparta (in southeastern Greece), for example, devoted the bulk of its national capital to its army, which became the strongest and most feared in Greece. So its artistic output, including the creation of large-scale public buildings, was minimal compared with that of a number of other states. In fact, architecturally speaking, Sparta became known for its outward simplicity and lack of ostentation. The fifth-century-B.C. Athenian historian Thucydides quipped that if Sparta

> were to become deserted and only the temples and foundations of buildings remained, I think that future generations would, as time passed, find it very difficult to believe that the place had really been as powerful as it was represented to be. Yet the Spartans occupy [a great deal of territory and have influence over many other Greek states]. Since, however, the city is not regularly planned and contains no temples or monuments of great magnificence, but is simply a collection of villages . . . its appearance would not come up to expectation.[16]

In contrast, Sparta's archrival, Athens (on the Attic peninsula, on Greece's east-central flank), in a very real sense chose statues over swords. The wealthiest and most populous city-state, Athens did have an army. But over time it spent as much or more on the arts than it did on defense. The result was that in the late Archaic Age, Athens produced an overall artistic output that became the envy of all other Greeks. Indeed, one of the main reasons the Athenians devoted so much money and energy to artistic projects was personal pride and the desire to impress the rest of Greece. Pericles (PAIR-uh-kleez), the city's leading statesman in the pivotal fifth century B.C., told his fellow citizens that their city was special, exceptional, and eternal. Moreover, he said, the gods had chosen it above all other countries. "You should fix your eyes every day on the greatness of Athens," he told them, "and should fall in love with her. When you realize her greatness, then reflect that what made her great was men with a spirit of adventure."[17]

The most visible aspect of Athens's artistic output was monumental architecture, which gave it (and any other state that could afford it) a look of grandeur, wealth, and importance. In particular, the Athenians, along with other Greeks, concentrated most on a particular kind of large-scale architecture—that of religious temples. This was partly because the classical Greeks were, at least initially, religiously devout. They believed that each city-state had a patron god or goddess who took a special interest in that community and its people. To ensure that one's divine patron would continue to show favor to that community, the people erected one or more temples in his or her honor. It was thought that the patron deity actually resided inside the temple from time to time. That is why public worship took place outside rather than inside a temple—to respect the god's privacy.

Athens was actually named for its holy patron, Athena, goddess of war and wisdom. To honor her, the fifth-century-B.C. Athenians constructed an immense and splendid complex of temples and other structures atop the Acropolis. Over time, these monuments became symbols not only of Athenian greatness, but also of Greek artistic genius in general. Pericles, the chief political supporter of the great project, actually sensed this would happen. "Future ages will wonder at us," he told his countrymen, "as the present age wonders at us now."[18]

Early Greek Temples

Before examining Athens's phenomenal achievement in temple construction, it must be established how the Athenians obtained the general design of these structures. The fact is that they did not invent Greek temple architecture's highly distinctive

A Goddess Aids an Architect?

In this passage from his encyclopedic work, the Natural History, *the noted Roman scholar Pliny the Elder discusses a quaint story related to the Greek architect Chersiphron. He designed the gigantic temple of Artemis at Ephesus, later listed as one of the Seven Wonders of the Ancient World.*

Chersiphron's greatest feat was his success in raising the architraves [horizontal stone slabs resting atop the columns] of this huge building into position. He achieved this by filling reed bags with sand and building a gently inclined ramp up to and above the level of the capitals [column-tops]. Then he gradually emptied the sacks at the bottom, so that the architrave gently settled into place. The greatest difficulty occurred as he tried to position the lintel [horizontal block] above the doors. This was the largest stone and refused to settle on its bed. Chersiphron was distraught and wondered [what to do]. The story goes that . . . in the middle of the night, while he slept, the goddess Artemis appeared to him [in a dream] and [said] she had laid the stone. Next day when it was light, this was seen to be true. The position of the stone appeared to have been corrected by its weight alone.

Pliny the Elder, *Natural History: A Selection.* Translated by John H. Healy. New York: Penguin, 1991, pp. 354–355.

look. That look developed gradually, beginning sometime between 900 to 700 B.C. (Scholars call that era, spanning the end of the Dark Age and opening of the Archaic Age, the geometric period of Greek art.)

Evidence shows that the earliest Greek temples were small, simple, hutlike structures made of wood, sun-dried mud bricks, and thatch (bundled tree branches). Because such materials are very perishable, none of these structures have survived. However, archaeologists have unearthed some small pottery models of them. One of these may represent an eighth-century-B.C. temple of Hera (wife of Zeus, leader of the gods). It featured a modest-sized front porch with a prominent pediment (the triangular gable beneath the end of the slanting roof). At the base of the pediment, just above the front door, was a horizontal beam—the architrave (or epistyle)—supported by two thin wooden columns.

In the years that followed, Greek architects considerably enlarged these structures, but they kept the basic structural elements, including porches, pediments, architraves, and columns. Of particular note, as their temples got longer, they added more and more columns and accordingly extended the architrave that sat atop them. Eventually, a colonnade (row of

The seventh-century B.C. Temple of Hera on Samos Island. Greek architects included basic structural elements such as porches, pediments, architraves, and columns in early designs.

columns) stretched along each of the structure's four sides. This unbroken perimeter of columns enclosing the rectangular building at the center is called a pteron (TAIR-on), and a building that employs it is said to be peripteral (puh-RIP-ter-ul). The builders also added a back porch with its own pediment to balance the front one. The first known peripteral temple of this kind was erected on the Aegean island of Samos in the early 700s B.C. Modern experts think it was more than 100 feet (30m) long, about 20 feet (6m) wide, and had forty-three wooden columns in its pteron.

The basic structural design of the Samian temple became more or less standard for the vast majority of Greek temples thereafter. But though these primary features were almost always present, the materials and construction methods the builders used continued to evolve. Changes in the roofing materials are a good example. Initially they had consisted of thick layers of thatch laid over a framework of wooden timbers. But as time went on, they were replaced with pottery roofing tiles.

Because the tiles were enormously heavy, the structure beneath them, including the vertical columns, had to be a great deal stronger than before. For a short while, architects called for using thicker wooden columns and other supporting elements. But as more and more decorations were added to the upper sections of temples, further increasing their weight, it became clear that wood would have to be abandoned in favor of stone. In the late 600s and early 500s B.C., therefore, architects and builders accomplished the laborious but necessary changeover to all-stone temples.

The First Two Architectural Orders

During the Archaic Age, when temple architecture was evolving and spreading across the Greek world, architects developed the first of three major architectural orders, or styles. Thereafter most of Greece's large-scale structures featured one (and on occasion two) of these styles. The earliest order was the Doric. As was the case with the other two styles, it was most easily identified by the distinctive features of its columns. Archaeologist Lesley Adkins explains:

> Doric columns had no base and rose directly from the floor, with a maximum diameter of about one-fifth or one-sixth the column height. . . . At the top of the column was a capital [topmost section] consisting of a basin-shaped circular molding and a plane square slab. The Doric order evolved in the 7th century B.C. and became the normal style in mainland Greece. . . . The main elements of a Doric building were the foundation . . . three steps up to the platform on which the structure was built, and the columns and their capital supporting the architrave.[19]

Directly above the architrave rested another distinctive feature of Doric temples—the Doric frieze. It consisted of a horizontal decorative band that was about the same thickness of the architrave and, like the latter, ran horizontally around the building's perimeter. A Doric frieze was not continuous. Instead, it was divided into separate rectangular panels, with every other panel adorned with either sculpted or painted figures.

The second major architectural order, the Ionic, developed in the Aegean Islands and in western Anatolia (now Turkey), which at the time was a Greek cultural region known as Ionia. According to scholar David Sacks:

> Lighter but more ornate than the Doric order, the Ionic employed certain distinctive details, the most obvious of which were the scroll-like volutes (or curls) at the four corners of the capital of each column. This lovely design may derive from the Tree of Life motif on [Middle] Eastern architecture, known to the Ionians through their trading contact with [cities and kingdoms in that region]. Ionic columns were more slender than their Doric counterparts. Other distinctive Ionic features included the use of a column base and the absence of [separated panels] along the frieze beneath the roof and pediments. Unlike the Doric [frieze], the Ionic [frieze] could show continuous carvings.[20]

Perhaps the most famous Ionic temple in the Greek lands was the one dedicated to Artemis, goddess of the moon and the hunt, at Ephesus (EF-uh-sis), in southern Ionia. The largest Greek temple ever erected, it was 377 feet (115m) long and 164 feet (50m) wide. According to the first-century-A.D. Roman scholar Pliny (PLIN-ee) the Elder, each of its enormous columns was 60 feet (20m) high. So impressive was this true work of architectural art that it came to be listed as one of the Seven Wonders of the Ancient World. Antipater (an-TIP-uh-ter) of Sidon, the second-century-B.C. Greek poet who compiled the list, first described the other six structures, then said of the seventh, the temple at Ephesus, "When I saw the sacred house of Artemis, that towers to the clouds, the other [wonders] were placed in the shade, for the sun himself has never looked upon its equal outside Olympus [the home of the Greek gods]."[21]

Part of the surviving remnants of the Ionic frieze on Athens's Parthenon show Athenian horsemen riding in a religious procession.

A reconstruction of the Temple of Artemis at Ephesus. The temple is an example of Ionic architecture and was one of the Seven Wonders of the Ancient World.

The Parthenon: Transporting the Stones

In contrast, the most impressive and famous Doric temple in the Greek sphere was the Parthenon, one of the temples erected in Pericles's great building program on the Athenian Acropolis. The Parthenon was built on roughly the same spot that an earlier Doric temple honoring Athena had stood. Specifically dedicated to Athena Polias (Athena "of the city"), it, along with other buildings on the Acropolis, had been destroyed in 480 B.C. when the Persians had invaded Greece. After driving away the invaders, the Athenians had left the ruins on the hill untouched. This was intended as a memorial to the war and Greece's salvation.

In the 440s B.C., however, Pericles and other ambitious leaders called for clearing the ruins and constructing a magnificent new temple complex in their place. No less than three new temples were to be constructed in Athena's honor. They were the small Temple of Athena Nike (Athena "the victor"), the medium-sized Erechtheum to house a special olive-wood statue of the goddess, and the huge Parthenon. (Surrounding these temples were a monumental gateway, the Propylaea; shrines to Artemis and other deities; and numerous statues of Athena and other gods.)

Indeed, from the very beginning the Parthenon was envisioned on a much larger scale than the average Doric temple. Most temples of this style had six columns each on the front and back porches and thirteen columns running along the sides. By contrast, the Parthenon's architects, Ictinus (ik-TY-nis) and Callicrates (kuh-LIK-ruh-teez), decided to utilize eight columns on each end and seventeen on each side. As a result, by default every facet of the building was bigger than normal. More than 22,000 tons (19,958t) of marble went into its construction, and it measured 237 feet (72m) long, 110 feet (33m) wide, and 65 feet (20m) high.

The erection of this architectural marvel, which a number of modern experts have called the most perfect building in history, began in Athens's main marble quarry on the side of Mount Pentelikon, about 10 miles (16.1km) northeast of Athens. First, workmen liberated each stone block from the mountainside. This was accomplished by using mallets and chisels to cut grooves in the marble, driving wooden wedges into the grooves, and saturating them with water. As the wedges absorbed the water, they expanded, forcing the stone to crack, after which the workers used crowbars and other tools to finish freeing the stones.

Other workers then loaded the stones onto wagons, and teams of oxen pulled the wagons to the Acropolis. These wagons were specially made larger than normal in order to bear the great weight of the blocks. Also, the builders created a stone causeway for part of the distance from the quarry to the city to eliminate the problem of the wagon wheels sinking into the ground.

Chersiphron (KUR-suh-frun), the architect who designed a large temple of Artemis at Ephesus, faced a similar challenge related to transporting stones. This structure was considerably

THE PARTHENON'S IONIC FRIEZE

British Museum scholar Ian Jenkins penned this description of some portions of the continuous Ionic frieze that Phidias and his assistants carved on the inside of the Parthenon's pteron. The carved scenes depicted Athenian citizens marching in Athens's largest yearly religious festival.

On the [building's] west side we see horsemen, some paired, others shown singly. The directional flow is from right to left, or south to north. . . . The long north side carries forward the cavalcade begun on the west, and the horsemen occupy nearly half of the total number of slabs. Ahead of them come chariots, then groups of figures walking in procession, including elders, musicians, pitcher-bearers, tray-bearers, and figures leading cattle and sheep as sacrificial victims. Turning the corner onto the east side we find . . . a procession of girls carrying [pottery] vessels [and] male figures leaning on staves [walking sticks] and engaged in conversation. . . . Ahead of them are shown the gods, whose seated pose allows them to appear larger than the mortal figures in the frieze. . . . The southern branch of the frieze follows a pattern similar to that of the north. The two processions do not actually meet, since the gods are placed between them.

Ian Jenkins. *The Parthenon Frieze*. Austin: University of Texas Press, 2002, pp. 22–24.

Sir Lawrence Alma-Tadema's painting depicts Phidias's interior Ionic frieze in the Parthenon's pteron.

larger than the Parthenon. So its stone blocks, including the individual pieces of the columns, called drums, were proportionally bigger and heavier than those in the Athenian temple. The first-century-B.C. Roman architect Vitruvius told how Chersiphron managed to solve this problem, saying:

> He distrusted his two-wheeled carts, fearing that the wheels [might] sink down in the yielding [soft-earthed] country lanes because of the huge loads. [So] he framed together four wooden pieces of four-inch timbers, two of them being cross-pieces as long as the stone column [drum]. At each end of the [drum] he ran in iron pivots with lead, dovetailing them, and fixed sockets in the wood frame to receive the pivots, binding the ends with wood [blocks]. Thus, the pivots fitted into the sockets and turned freely.[22]

Thus, Chersiphron rigged the circular column drums so they would roll along the ground like super-thick wheels of a huge wagon. A team of oxen tied to the wooden framework provided the power. The beauty of this brilliant contraption was that each drum was at least 3 feet (1m) thick, so its weight was spread out across a much wider area than the relatively thin wheel of a standard wagon. Consequently, the drums did not sink into the ground as the wagon wheels would have.

The Culmination of Culture

Whether it was the Ephesus temple, the Parthenon, or any other Greek temple, once the marble blocks reached the work site, stonemasons went to work. They used chisels and other tools to dress (trim and polish) the blocks so that they would fit into premeasured spaces in the rising building. This work had to be done as accurately as possible because, with few exceptions, Greek builders did not use mortar in large structures. Rather, the blocks fit together tightly, after which workers joined one to another with I-shaped iron clamps that lay inside chiseled recesses. When the next course of blocks was laid above, it covered and hid the clamps in the course below.

The stonemasons also dressed the rounded drums for the columns. A typical column on the Parthenon consisted of a stack of eleven drums. As in the case of the wall blocks, adjoining column drums were held together by recessed metal fasteners that were later hidden by the drums stacked above them.

Lifting the upper drums, as well as the blocks for the upper courses of the Parthenon's walls, was achieved using simple but effective mechanical hoists. The most common version consisted of a wooden framework rigged with a clever arrangement of ropes and pulleys. Once the proper rope from the hoist was attached to the block, teams of oxen or men pulled on the rope, raising the block toward its final resting place. Lastly, a small team of workers guided the block to that place and used crowbars to make an exact fit.

When the walls, columns, architraves, roof, and other structural elements were all in place, other artists began decorating the

The Parthenon in Athens, Greece.

CURVES THAT LOOKED STRAIGHT

The architects who designed the Parthenon employed a number of subtle architectural corrections, or refinements, when raising the structure. This was because they knew from experience that in large buildings perfectly straight lines frequently look curved, rather than straight, to the human eye. For instance, long horizontal floor or roof lines can seem to slump downward a bit in the middle. The refinements that Ictinus and Callicrates called for in their plans were meant to compensate for such optical illusions. In some cases this was done by exaggerating various curves and other visual proportions to fool the eye into thinking it was seeing straight lines. The builders made the Parthenon's column shafts swell slightly in the middle, for example, an effect called entasis. This counteracted a tendency for straight vertical lines to look thinner in the middle and thereby weak. In addition, all the columns in the temple's pteron leaned inward slightly, providing the temple with a look of amplified soaring perspective. In still other refinements, the building's floor curved upward in a gentle arc, and some of the panels in the Doric frieze had no straight lines, although they looked perfectly straight when viewed from ground level. The Parthenon's refinements were implemented with phenomenal accuracy, their overall margin of error being less than 0.25 inches (0.64cm).

enormous edifice. Beautiful sculptures were added to each of the Doric frieze's alternating panels, called metopes (MET-uh-peez). Also, in a unique move not seen in prior Doric temples, an Ionic frieze filled with sculptures was carved in a continuous band located on the inside of the architrave and Doric frieze, facing the central building. (The public could barely see this second frieze, even when standing up against the building's walls. The consensus of modern experts is that it was intended more for the gods than for humans to see.)

Also, collections of larger-than-life-sized statues were placed inside the pediments at the ends of the structure, each group representing a dramatic scene from mythology. Meanwhile, painters applied bright colors (mostly red, blue, and gold) to selected portions of the temple. At the same time, the great Athenian sculptor Phidias (FID-ee-us), who designed all of the building's carved figures, crafted a gigantic statue of Athena in the main interior chamber, or cella.

The Parthenon's overall combination of architectural, sculptural, and decorative excellence produced a genuine triumph of artistic splendor. Countless visitors to the Acropolis over the centuries have confirmed this judgment, including one who exclaimed, "All the world's culture culminated in Greece, all Greece in Athens, all Athens in its Acropolis, all the Acropolis in the Parthenon."[23]

Other Major Architectural Forms

For most people today, standard Doric and Ionic temples are the most recognizable large-scale architectural forms from ancient Greece. The Greeks had many other kinds of monumental buildings, however. These included nonstandard, or atypical, temples; giant gateways; storehouses for valuables; town halls; theaters; and several others. Many of these forms utilized Doric or Ionic pillars and decorations, giving them a decidedly Greek look. That look was so elegant and attractive that other peoples readily borrowed it, especially the Romans, who were thoroughly seduced by almost all forms of Greek art.

Tombs of Society's Elite

One kind of large-scale structure used intermittently across the Greek lands from the Bronze Age to the close of ancient times was the monumental tomb. Expensive and ambitious projects, these were always erected for kings, queens, nobles, and other wealthy and important members of society's elite. The first notable examples were built in mainland Greece by the Mycenaeans beginning in about 1550 B.C. These large conical- or dome-shaped structures, called *tholoi* (THOH-loy), were constructed of courses of big, rough-hewn stones. Each course

The largest *tholos* yet discovered is the Treasury of Atreus at Mycenae. The people in the picture give scale to the structure, which is 48 feet in diameter and 43 feet in height.

tilted inward slightly and overlapped the one before it until the narrowing courses formed a dome. Because they looked similar to the conical containers used by beekeepers, these domed chambers also became known as "beehive tombs." When a *tholos* was completed, the builders covered it with an enormous mound of dirt known as a tumulus. In the years that followed, the dead were laid either on low platforms on the dirt floor or in graves dug into that floor.

The largest *tholos* discovered to date is the Treasury of Atreus, lying just outside the palace compound at Mycenae. (The word *treasury* was coined in a later age by people who mistakenly thought it was a storehouse for valuables.) The tomb's interior chamber is some 48 feet (15m) in diameter and 43 feet (13m) high. One of the stones, lying horizontally above the inner door, weighs about 100 tons (90.7t). Evidence shows that the tomb was originally elegantly decorated, with painted columns flanking the entranceway and numerous painted plaques lining the inside of the dome.

The Greeks constructed few large, highly ornamented tombs in the Archaic and Classical ages, but in early Hellenistic times these structures became more numerous. The reason was that Archaic and Classical Greece were dominated by city-states, in which the nobility declined in favor of elected officials. This was especially true in the many democratic states that followed the lead of the world's first democracy—Athens. In the Hellenistic Age, by contrast, the most powerful states were large kingdoms with entrenched royal families and landed nobles. These followed the lead of Macedonia, in northern Greece, which rose to prominence under King Philip II, father of Alexander III, later called "Alexander the Great."

Indeed, a group of tombs belonging to Macedonian nobles found in the 1970s at Vergina, the site of ancient Macedonia's capital, Aegae, are impressive. One is believed by some experts to be that of Philip himself. However, some recent evidence suggests that the cremated body in question may be that of Alexander's young half brother, Philip III, who briefly inherited the throne after Alexander's untimely death in 323 B.C. The late noted British scholar A.W. Lawrence remarked that this tomb, "with its lavish furnishings of gold and silver and bronze, arms and armor, and the decayed remains of fabric and furniture, constitutes one of the most spectacular archaeological discoveries in Greece. It is also important for its contribution to our understanding of Greek architecture."[24]

Architecturally speaking, the main section of the tomb consists of a stone burial vault measuring 31 feet (9.5m) long and 18 feet (5.5m) wide. Commenting on the tomb's artistic qualities, Greek historian Vlasis Vlasidis writes that the facade on the front has the form of a Doric temple, with a marble door, and is adorned with [a small Doric frieze]. Above the Doric frieze, however, there is an Ionic frieze with a painting of a hunting scene. Three horsemen and seven men on foot pursue a lion, deer, and boar. Only one of the men is mature and bearded, and he [has been] identified [by some experts] as Philip. Another of the men [may be] Alexander. . . . In the burial chamber was found a marble sarcophagus, inside which was a gold larnax [box for cremated remains] containing the ashes of the dead king and his crown . . . together with [the] remains of [a] wooden mortuary couch adorned with gold, glass, and ivory.[25]

The entrance to tombs belonging to Macedonian nobles was unearthed at Vergina in the 1970s.

The Magnificent Mausoleum

Although the Macedonian tombs were spacious and carefully decorated by artists, they were not large enough to qualify as monumental structures. However, a number of enormous grave monuments were constructed in Greek-speaking lands in the same period and on into Hellenistic times. The largest and most famous was the Mausoleum at Halicarnassus, which Antipater of Sidon placed on his list of the world's seven wonders along with the Temple of Artemis at Ephesus.

The term *mausoleum*, which today means "a large tomb," is derived from *Mausolus* (MAW-so-lus), the name of the king

In building her husband's mausoleum, Artemisia hired Greek architects Satyros and Pythis to design it and employed the best known Greek sculptors of the day to decorate it.

whose remains were put to rest in the great monument. Mausolus ruled Caria, a kingdom that stretched across southwestern Anatolia, including Halicarnassus and other Ionian cities. He greatly admired Greek culture and established several new towns with public buildings in Greek architectural styles. Naturally enough, he also desired to be buried in a tomb designed by Greek architects. To that end, when he died in 353 B.C. his beloved sister and wife, Artemisia, who oversaw the Mausoleum's construction, hired two noted Greek architects, Satyros and Pythis (or Pythius). She also employed four of the best-known Greek sculptors of the day to decorate the tomb—Scopas, Bryaxis, Timotheus, and Leochares.

A number of ancient writers described the completed Mausoleum, including Pliny the Elder. "It is 63 feet long on the north and south sides [but] shorter on the façades," he said, adding that it had thirty-six columns holding up its pyramid-shaped roof.

> The sculptures on the east side were carved by Scopas, those on the north by Bryaxis, those on the south by Timotheus, and those on the west by Leochares. . . . Above the colonnade is a pyramid, equal in height to the lower part, [and there are] 24 steps to the topmost point. On the summit is a marble four-horse chariot made by Pythis. When this is included [in the structure's measurements], it brings the whole building to a height of 140 feet.[26]

Studies by archaeologists have confirmed that most of Pliny's claims were correct or almost so. They estimate that the tomb's total height was 148 feet (45m) and say that there was indeed a larger-than-life sculpture of a chariot drawn by four horses on the top. The chariot contained male and female statues said to represent Mausolus and Artemisia. Regrettably, these sculptures, as well as the Mausoleum itself, no longer exist. One of antiquity's greatest architectural masterpieces, the building lasted about sixteen centuries until it finally toppled in a large earthquake sometime in the thirteenth century. In the decades that followed, most of the fallen blocks were used in the construction of a nearby medieval castle. However, modern excavators were able to recover some fragments of columns and statues of gods from the Mausoleum. They also found a panel of carved figures from a frieze by one of the sculptors who worked on the project.

An Architect for the Ages

*A*mong the greatest of Greece's architects in the fifth century B.C. was Ictinus, one of the two designers of the immortal Parthenon. That feat alone made him a sort of architect for the ages. Almost nothing is known about his personal life. But various ancient writers confirmed that he was responsible for some of the finest classical Greek buildings. In addition to the Parthenon, the second-century-A.D. traveler Pausanias wrote, Ictinus created the Temple of Apollo at Bassae, in the central part of the Peloponnesus (the large peninsula making up mainland Greece's southern third). The building was known for being the first Greek structure to feature a Corinthian column, as well as for its great beauty. Pausanias wrote, "Of all the temples in the Peloponnesus, this one could be considered second only to the temple at Tegea for its proportions and the beauty of its stone." Ictinus also designed the Doric Temple of Hephaestus in Athens and the Telesterion, the large structure in Eleusis (west of Athens), in which the members of the cult of Demeter met and viewed their secret sacred objects. Many centuries later, noted French painter Jean-Auguste-Dominique Ingres honored Ictinus in a canvas, now in London's National Gallery, that shows the ancient architect talking to the Greek poet Pindar.

Pausanias. *Guide to Greece*, Vol. 2. Translated by Peter Levi. New York: Penguin, 1971, p. 474.

Monumental Gateways

More substantial sections of some of ancient Greece's numerous public architectural forms have survived. Among them are versions of the *propylon* (PROP-uh-lon), or monumental gateway. Its principal use was as a formal entranceway into a city or the sacred sanctuary surrounding a temple. The most famous *propylon* is the Propylaea (prop-uh-LEE-uh), on the western flank of the Athenian Acropolis. It was designed by the architect Mnesikles (NES-uh-kleez) as part of the grand fifth-century-B.C. building program on that hill.

A person of that era who set out to climb to the Acropolis's summit first ascended several marble ramps that zigzagged upward toward the great gateway. About halfway up, he or she could see to the right the small Temple of Athena Nike, resting on a stone rampart that thrust outward from the hill. Climbing two more ramps brought the person to the Propylaea. It was shaped like a huge T, with its stem projecting inward toward the summit. Inside the stem was a long hallway bordered by columns that supported a gabled roof like that of a temple. The T's wings, facing the climber, consisted of rectangular structures sitting at right angles to the central hallway. The right, south-facing wing nestled a few feet behind the Temple of Athena Nike, while the left, north-facing wing contained an art gallery where some of Athens's finest painters hung their works.

Designed by the architect Mnesikles, the Propylaea is the entrance to the Acropolis and is the most famous example of the *propylon,* or monumental gate.

When the person walked through the hallway at the heart of the gateway and emerged on the summit, he or she immediately caught sight of the glorious Parthenon positioned about 260 feet (80m) away toward the right. This was no accident. Mnesikles purposely aligned the Propylaea so that the stem of its T was parallel to the Parthenon's long axis. "The Propylaea and Parthenon, with their parallel axes," William R. Biers points out, "were obviously part of the same general plan. The space around the Parthenon was [kept clear] so that the first view of it from the Propylaea would be impressive."[27]

Atypical Temples

After drinking in the stunning sight of the looming Parthenon, the person turned slightly and saw off to the left the Acropolis's third temple—the Erechtheum (or Erechtheion). What made the Erechtheum visually striking in its own right

A bird's-eye view of a reconstruction of the Athenian Acropolis.

was its highly unusual, even unexpected, design. In fact, it was the best known of Greece's atypical temples. Because these buildings did not follow the rules of standard temple design, they constituted separate architectural forms unto themselves.

An Ionic structure, the Erechtheum featured four porches, one each on its north, south, east, and west sides. They were part of a unique, deliberately asymmetrical, split-level layout. "These porches," Lawrence explained, "differ tremendously in all three dimensions and rise from very different levels." The north porch "is larger in every respect." Yet the south porch, though considerably smaller, is even more eye-catching. "Instead of columns," Lawrence continued, "it is supported by statues of women."[28] Six in number, these sculpture-pillars, called *karyatids* (kar-ee-AH-tidz), gave the south porch its popular name—the Porch of the Maidens. (The *karyatids* seen on the temple today are replicas. To save them from further weathering, the originals now rest in various museums.)

Other atypical temples could be found in various Greek city-states and kingdoms. Of two that were familiar to most Greeks, the first was the Athenian Temple of Apollo on the Aegean island of Delos, erected in the late fifth century B.C. It had no pteron. Instead, six Doric columns stood in front, another six in back, and in the rear of the front porch stood four square piers (vertical structural supports) instead of circular columns. The second widely familiar atypical temple was built in honor of Athena at Delphi, in south-central Greece. A rare round temple, it measured 43 feet (13.5m) across and featured a circular colonnade with twenty Doric columns.

Other Common Public Buildings

Of the other common forms of public building in ancient Greece, two externally resembled small standard Doric or Ionic temples but had little or nothing to do with religion. One of these forms was an attractive, usually artistically elaborate structure known as a treasury. Greek treasuries were used to store various valuables. It was customary, for instance, for people to give

On the other side of the Athenian Acropolis rests another splendid ancient Greek theater —the Odeon of Herodes Atticus, built in A.D. 161. In both ancient times and today the theater is used for musical concerts.

*A*mong the many architectural forms the Greeks pioneered were the world's first theaters. Earliest of all was one erected in Athens in the late sixth century B.C. In 499 B.C. its wooden seating section collapsed, killing many spectators, and it was therefore abandoned. The theater that soon replaced it—the Theater of Dionysus—underwent periodic changes and improvements over the course of several centuries. By the mid-400s B.C. it featured a circular "dancing place," also called the orchestra, where the actors performed. Arrayed in a large semicircle in front of the orchestra were rows of ascending bleachers. At first they were made of wood and built into the earth on the southeastern slope of the Acropolis, but these were later replaced by stone seats. The seating capacity eventually reached an estimated fourteen thousand. On the opposite side of the orchestra from the seats was the *skene*, or "scene building," a long, narrow structure that tripled as a surface on which to paint background settings for the plays, a dressing room for the players, and storage space for props. Today the Theater of Dionysus lies in an advanced state of ruin. But the theater at Epidaurus (southwest of Athens), erected in the 300s B.C., is so well preserved that Greece's National Theater stages plays there each year.

gifts, some of them expensive, to gods at religious sanctuaries and temples. Priests collected these offerings and stored them in nearby treasuries. These structures were also intended to flaunt the wealth, power, and religious devotion of the Greek states that built them. Consequently, numerous states erected treasuries at places where people from all across Greece gathered on special occasions, including Delphi, home of the renowned oracle (a priestess thought to be a medium between the god Apollo and humans). Another was Olympia (in southwestern Greece), home of the famous ancient athletic games.

A second public structure that looked like a small temple was the fountain house. A water distribution center, it was most often built next to a stream or aqueduct and stored water from one of those sources. People who lived in the general vicinity utilized spigots protruding from an outer wall to draw water, which they carted away in buckets.

Although they did not look anything like temples, Greek halls did frequently feature Doric or Ionic elements, including columns. Halls, almost always located in urban centers, acted as public meeting places. A majority were used for political purposes, especially for meetings of town officials, while some hosted public banquets or religious gatherings. A typical hall was square-shaped, with a decorative row of columns in the front porch and often several rows of pillars evenly spaced for structural support in the interior. Today, the best-known public hall from ancient Greece is the council-house at Athens. Dating from the fifth century B.C., it measured 78.0 by 76.5 feet (24m by 23m).

The council-house was located on the edge of Athens's main marketplace, the Agora. In that same district, as well as in numerous other areas across Greece where large numbers of people gathered, stood examples of another important form of public building. Known as a stoa, it was a long, relatively narrow structure featuring a roofed walkway in front. Supporting the roof was a row of graceful columns. On the inside, parallel with the columns, was a line of a dozen or more rooms, used variously as workrooms for artisans and/or merchants' stalls.

Thus, stoas were sometimes like miniature shopping malls. At the same time, the roofed walkways of stoas provided places for citizens to find shelter from a sudden rainstorm or the hot afternoon sun. Over time, stoas also served as meeting places for informal political and philosophical discussions and educational lectures.[29]

Hellenistic Developments

In addition, during the Hellenistic Age the Greeks started using stoas to aid in efficient town planning and traffic control ("traffic" here meaning human pedestrians, wagons, and animals). According to Biers, "In the second century B.C. the Athenian Agora took on a more ordered look, with stoas defining the south and east boundaries. This use of the stoa to surround or define a space reflects the [Hellenistic] interest in space and planning. Stoas played a great part in the unified complexes that are found where new Hellenistic cities or sanctuaries were laid out."[30]

Another of the building-related developments of Hellenistic times was a widening use of the third major architectural order, the Corinthian. It first appeared in the late fifth century B.C., after the Doric and Ionic orders had been employed for some time. But the Greeks applied it only rarely until the early years of the Hellenistic Age. The first important Greek structure with Corinthian columns on its exterior was the Choragic Monument of Lysicrates (ly-SIK-rah-teez) in Athens, erected in 334 B.C. A circular edifice sitting on a tall, square-shaped podium, it was built to celebrate the victory of the wealthy Athenian citizen Lysicrates. The play he had financially backed that year had won the city's yearly drama contest.

Of the three Greek orders, the Corinthian is more ornate and stylish than the other two. The capital of a Corinthian column is adorned with a mass of graceful masonry leaves, said to imitate those of the acanthus plant. Especially in ancient times, when painted gold or silver, these capitals conveyed feelings of imperial majesty and splendor. So although the Romans borrowed all three orders from the Greeks for their own

The Monument of
Lysicrates in Athens
was built in 334 B.C.
and is an early
example of the
Corinthian order.

ORIGINS OF THE CORINTHIAN ORDER

The first-century-B.C. Roman architect Vitruvius offered the following story, likely a folktale, of how the third Greek architectural order—the Corinthian—developed.

The first invention of that [style of column] capital is related to have happened thus. A girl, a native of Corinth, already of age to be married, was attacked by disease and died. After her funeral, the goblets which delighted her when living, were put together in a basket by her nurse, carried to the [burial] monument, and placed on the top. That they might remain longer, exposed as they were to the weather, she covered the basket with a tile. As it happened, the basket was placed upon the root of an acanthus [plant]. Meanwhile, about springtime, the root of the acanthus, being pressed down in the middle by the weight, put forth leaves and shoots. The shoots grew up the sides of the basket [and formed] the curves of volutes at the extreme parts. Then [the sculptor] Callimachus . . . was passing [by] the monument [and] perceived the basket and the young leaves growing up. Pleased with the style . . . he made columns for the Corinthians on this model and [settled on the correct] proportions [for the new order].

Vitruvius. *On Architecture*, Vol. 1. Translated by Frank Granger. Cambridge, MA: Harvard University Press, 2002, p. 209.

public buildings, they particularly liked and widely used the Corinthian. For that reason, although the Greeks invented the order, it came to be associated more with the Romans.

A particularly dramatic and beautiful Greek architectural form that became popular in the Hellenistic era was the monumental stepped altar. The Greeks had employed outdoor altars for religious purposes (especially for sacrificing animals) for many centuries. But these structures, most often made of stone, were usually on the small side, ranging from 4 to 10 feet (1.2m to 3.0m) wide and no higher than a person's waist.

By contrast, some Hellenistic altars were expanded into enormous stone platforms resting atop massive staircases. The finest artists embellished them with paint, statues, and friezes containing magnificent sculpted figures. One of the biggest and by far the most renowned monumental altar of the Hellenistic Greek lands was the Great Altar of Zeus. Erected by Eumenes II, ruler of the kingdom of Pergamum (PUR-ga-mum) in northwestern Anatolia, it was part of that monarch's splendid acropolis complex in his capital (also called Perga-mum). Some 120 feet (36.5m) wide and 112 feet (34m) deep, the altar featured a marble staircase 65 feet (20m) wide; two huge wings that projected outward, encasing the staircase; and an Ionic frieze 371 feet (113m) long showing a mythical scene of gods fighting giants. Today, the Pergamum altar is often ranked with the Parthenon and Artemis's temple at Ephesus as one of the three great pinnacles of ancient Greek architectural genius and grandeur.

4

Beyond Nature: Greek Sculpture

E ven as monumental architecture steadily spread across the Greek lands during the late Archaic Age (circa 700–500 B.C.), Greek sculptors began to perfect their art. They did not produce the kind of amazingly lifelike statues their successors would in the Classical and Hellenistic ages to come. Most late Archaic Greek figures, carved mostly from stone, are stiff- and formal-looking and lack realistic detail. Still, they are elegant and compelling artworks in their own right. Also, they consti- tute an important link in the sculptural chain from the Dark Age, which produced little or no sculpture (nor other arts); to the early Archaic Age (the eighth century B.C.), when sculp- tors made mostly small, crude figurines from bronze and stone; to the glorious larger-than-life-sized sculptures of Classical and Hellenistic times. Nigel Spivey points out:

> We will embark on a tale of technical exploration that takes us from [small rudimentary carvings] to full-scale and sophisticated, naturalistic statues. . . . Greek art was driven by a collective desire on the part of artists to pro- duce ever more realistic-looking figures. Moreover, [there] was an unusually accelerated change in the style of [sculpted figures] in Greece over the course of little more than 200 years.[31]

Late Archaic Statues

The major achievement of Greek sculptors in the late Archaic era consisted of life-sized human figures that were clearly influenced by Egyptian statues. The latter were more often than not in standing poses, somewhat stiff, and had one leg advanced slightly in front of the other. The late art historian Thomas Craven described their archaic Greek counterparts. In the male statues, he said, "the long arms hung down close to the slim-waisted body. The left foot was advanced in Egyptian style, and the face bore a curious smile—the Archaic style that captivated [the great Renaissance artist] Leonardo da Vinci. The first [carved Greek] women were in the shape of marble columns . . . motionless, the legs pressed together."[32]

The *kouros* of Anavysos, 530 B.C., is an example of the late Archaic period of Greek sculpture, which had grown more realistic in its depiction of the human form.

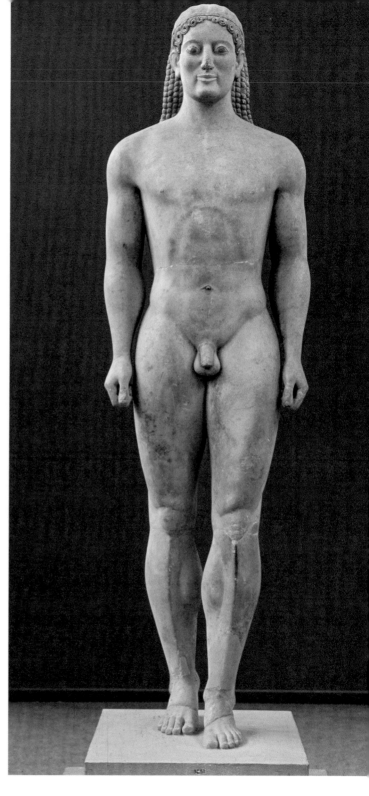

The male statues Craven mentioned were called *kouroi* (KOU-ree or KOU-roi, "young men"), and the female ones *korai* (KOR-ay, "maidens"). Although their stiff standing pose remained unchanged for almost a century, toward the close of the Archaic period these sculptures grew somewhat more realistic. This important change can be seen in the so-called Anavysos *kouros*, on display in Athens's National Archaeological Museum. Although its body is fairly stiff, as in traditional *kouroi*, it has considerably more detail, including the depiction of tear ducts.

Early Classical Figures

The stylistic changes seen in Greece's late Archaic carved figures suddenly speeded up in the early years of the Classical Age. By 480 to 470 B.C., in the immediate aftermath of the failed large-scale Persian invasion of Greece, a major transition in Greek sculpture was in full swing. Noted classical scholar Thomas R. Martin explains:

> New poses became ever more prevalent in free-standing sculpture, continuing an earlier evolution toward [realism]. Their postures and their physiques were evolving toward ever more naturalistic renderings. While Archaic male statues had been made striding forward with their left legs . . . male statues might now have bent arms or the body's weight on either leg. Their musculature was anatomically correct rather than sketchy and almost impressionistic, as had been the style [before]. Female statues, too, now had more relaxed poses and clothing.[33]

As the Classical Age continued, sculptural styles increasingly moved not only toward naturalism, but eventually beyond it. Sculptors strove for and achieved larger-than-life qualities of beauty, grace, and nobility. This produced what came to be called the "classical ideal." "From the mastery of movement and anatomy," Craven wrote, "artists proceeded to ideal forms and faces—to the creation of figures, male and female, beyond those produced by nature [which led] to their

THE FIRST PUBLIC STATUES

Many of the finest statues the Greeks produced were images of the winners of athletic competitions, although statues of other public figures were carved as well. In this excerpt from his famous encyclopedia of natural history, the first-century-A.D. Roman scholar Pliny the Elder describes the beginnings of the tradition of creating such statues.

ikenesses of men were not usually made [in those days] unless they deserved lasting commemoration for some outstanding reason, such as a victory in the sacred games, particularly those held at Olympia, where it was customary to dedicate statues of all winners. When an individual had won three times, exact likenesses were made of him, and these were known as "portrait statues." The first portrait statues erected at public expense in Athens were probably those of the [tyrant-killers] Harmodius and Arsitogiton. . . . Out of a most civilized sense of rivalry, the setting up of statues [by the Greeks] was afterwards adopted by the whole world. The custom arose of having statues adorn the forums [town squares] in all municipal towns, and . . . the memory of men was perpetuated by inscribing rolls of honor on statue bases to be read for all time.

Pliny the Elder, *Natural History: A Selection.* Translated by John H. Healy. New York: Penguin, 1991, pp. 310–311.

great masterpieces—to marbles which reveal living flesh within the polished surfaces, faces of god-like serenity, women in costumes of infinite grace."[34]

The classical sculptors carved both freestanding statues and figures mounted on or carved into the surfaces of temples and other buildings. Of the freestanding ones, many were displayed on the grounds of major religious sanctuaries, such as those at

Myron's statue of a drunken old woman holding a wineskin. Myron was said to make statues so realistic that they seemed ready to pull free of their bases and walk away.

Olympia and Delphi. One of the great specialists in freestanding figures in the pivotal fifth century B.C. was Myron (MY-ron or MEE-ron), an Athenian who worked mostly in bronze and produced numerous statues of leading athletes. He was said to have the ability to make statues of people so realistic that they seemed ready to pull free of their bases and walk away. Exemplifying this quality is a surviving fifth-century-B.C. verse about

Myron, who flourished in the fifth century B.C., was said to have been one of classical Greece's finest sculptors. The first-century-A.D. Roman scholar Pliny the Elder gave this brief overview of what little was known about him in Pliny's own time:

M yron, [a] pupil of [the sculptor] Hagelades, was born at Eleutherae [north of Athens]. His statue of a calf brought him particular fame. This was celebrated by some verses. . . . His other works include Ladas, the Discus-thrower (the Discobolos), [and] Perseus and the Sawyers. . . . Myron seems to be the first sculptor to have extended the scope of realism. There was more harmony in his art than in [that of earlier sculptors], and he exercised more care with regard to proportions.[1]

Among the verses about Myron's calf mentioned by Pliny were these: "Either a hide completely of bronze provides the covering for a real cow, or the bronze has a soul within it"; "Seeing the calf of Myron, you would quickly cry out: Nature is

lifeless but art is alive!"; and "For those who behold it, art has stolen the powers of nature!"[2]

1. Pliny the Elder, *Natural History: A Selection*. Translated by John H. Healy. New York: Penguin, 1991, p. 315.
2. From the *Greek Anthology*. Quoted in J.J. Pollitt, ed. and trans. *The Art of Ancient Greece: Sources and Documents*. New York: Cambridge University Press, 1990, p. 50.

In Myron's Discobolus (discus-thrower), the sculptor shows his attention to the details of human anatomy. Unlike sculptors before him, Myron exercised great care in regard to anatomical proportions.

Myron's incredibly realistic statue of a victorious sprinter named Ladas. The anonymous poem reads:

> As you once were, O Ladas, full of life, when you left behind wind-swift Thymos [a rival runner], straining your sinews as you ran on the tip of your toes. So did Myron cast you in bronze, and stamp everywhere on your body your anticipation of the [victor's] crown [made of laurel leaves]. He [the statue] is full of hope, and on the edge of his lips the breath from his hollow flanks is visible. Soon the bronze will leap for the crown, nor will the [stone] base be able to hold it back. Oh, art is swifter than a breath of wind.[35]

Of the bronze and/or stone statues that adorned temples and other monumental structures, some of the finest examples from the fifth century B.C. were created for the Parthenon, on Athens's Acropolis. Both of its pediments bore groups of stone statues, roughly twenty-two in each group. The figures in the front, or western, pediment portrayed the mythical contest between the deities Athena and Poseidon to decide which would become the city's patron. (Athena won.) The sculptures in the rear, or eastern, pediment depicted the famous myth in which Athena sprang, clad in full armor, from the head of her divine father, Zeus. Other figures graced the Parthenon's friezes, which bore extensive reliefs (or bas-reliefs), carvings raised partly from the flat surfaces. Some of these figures appeared in the metopes in the Doric frieze above the architrave, while others were fashioned in the continuous Ionic frieze located behind and above the pteron.

Creating Carved Figures

Whether a sculptor set out to make a freestanding stone statue or a stone figure portrayed in relief, the first step was to make a small clay model. Major sculptors like Myron and his Athenian colleague Phidias sometimes made such models themselves, but more often they had assistants do them. The chief sculptor, or master, probably gave the assistant a sketch to work from and later approved the model (or asked for changes in it). Then the assistants fashioned a full-sized clay model for each planned sculpted figure.

When the actual stone carving began, the master, while eyeing the full-sized model closely, made marks on the blank stone block to indicate where the carving should begin. Then the assistants chipped away the initial layers of marble until the figure's basic proportions were roughed in. From there, the master took over and provided the final proportions and details.

The tools wielded by both master sculptors and their assistants included metal chisels of various shapes and widths. The artist held one against the marble in the desired spot and struck the back of the chisel with a wooden mallet, producing a stone chip that fell to the floor. The same process was used for pointed tools, appropriately called points (or punches). Ancient sculptors also employed assorted drills. One of the latter, the auger, was one of the most versatile instruments in the sculptor's tool box. About it, the late German scholar Carl Bluemel said:

> It is the simplest of tools . . . nothing more than a sharp, flat chisel, terminating in a short point. It is whirled between the palms of the hands and bores holes in the stone. In order to put more power behind it, the tool is usually given the cranked form of a joiner's drill with a large round knob or grip. The sculptor can then brace it against his chest and revolve it with his hand. . . . The long, narrow grooves or folds, especially, can be more easily worked with a drill than with any other tool, because holes may be drilled close together and the small sections of stone remaining between them can then be removed [with another tool].[36]

The final step in the process required the input of other artists and craftsmen, including metalworkers and painters. They decorated and accessorized the finished sculptures that adorned the Parthenon and other buildings. The painters coated

A nineteenth-century painting depicts the studio of Phidias.

the figures with wax and bright-colored paint. When it dried, the wax had a yellowish-brown tinge that gave the flesh sections of human statues the look of sun-tanned skin. Hair, lips, and eyebrows were painted a deep red. The painters also applied varying shades of red, blue, and yellow to the clothes of the carved human figures. Meanwhile, the metalworkers made bronze spears, horse harnesses, and other implements and fitted them into small holes the sculptors had drilled in the appropriate spots, all following the master's initial design.

The Giant Image of Athena

Many of the sculptures that appeared in the pediments of the Parthenon and other temples, along with freestanding statues placed around these and other structures, were either life-sized or somewhat larger. A few classical Greek sculptors also created giant statues, ranging from 15 to 40 feet (4.5 to 12.2m) or more in height. These were usually intended as cult images—statues of gods that stood inside temples. However, some, like a huge figure of Athena—the *Athena Promachos*—on the Athenian Acropolis, stood outside in public view.

The designer of the *Athena Promachos*, Phidias, is now widely recognized as the greatest sculptor of ancient times. Almost nothing is known about his early life, except that he was born in about 490 B.C., the year in which his countrymen defeated a large Persian army at Marathon (lying northeast of Athens's urban center). Phidias later became a close friend of the Athenian statesman Pericles, who in the 440s B.C. enlisted him to take charge of creating sculptures for the new Parthenon.

This work entailed not only the large figures for the pediments and the relief sculptures for the metopes, but also the giant cult image of Athena, the *Athena Parthenos*, which dominated the temple's cella. No traces of this colossal, magnificent creation, which stood nearly 40 feet (12.2m) high, have survived. But various evidence, including miniature copies (originally sold to ancient tourists visiting Athens) and written descriptions, give a fairly good approximation of what it looked like. One of the written accounts is that of the second-century-A.D. Greek traveler Pausanias, who said:

> The statue is made of ivory and gold. She [Athena] has a sphinx on the middle of her helmet, and griffins worked on either side of it. . . . The griffins are wild monsters like lions with wings and the beak of an eagle, but this is enough about griffins. The statue of Athena stands upright in an ankle-length tunic with the head of Medusa [a mythical monster with snakes for hair] carved in ivory on her breast[plate]. She [Athena] has a [statue of the goddess] Victory about eight feet high [in one hand] and a spear in her [other] hand, and a shield at her feet, and a snake beside the shield. . . . The plinth [pedestal] of the statue is carved with the birth of Pandora. [The epic poet] Hesiod and others say Pandora was the first woman ever born.[37]

This modern reconstruction shows Phidias and Pericles consulting on Phidias's creation of the *Athena Parthenos*, a gigantic statue in the interior of the Parthenon.

On the surfaces of the statue's huge shield, Phidias carved detailed and dramatic battle scenes in relief. On the outside was a skirmish between the Athenians and the Amazons, a famous mythical race of warrior women. The inside of the shield bore a depiction of the Gigantomachy (gee-gan-TOM-uh-kee), a mythical battle between Zeus and his Olympian gods and a race of murderous giants. This scene earned the sculptor sharp criticism, according to the first-century-A.D. Greek biographer Plutarch. The story goes that some people accused Phidias of disrespecting the goddess by making two of the

PHIDIAS SUSPECTED OF SHADY DEALINGS

Noted classical historian Peter Green here explains how, not long after the Parthenon was finished, Phidias, who had designed its many sculptures, including the giant statue of Athena that stood inside, was suspected of embezzling some of the funds raised to pay for the project.

Over 2,500 pounds of gold—worth more than 3,500,000 drachmas —had gone into it, and another 1,386,000 drachmas had been expended on ivory, wood, sculptors' fees, and miscellaneous expenses. . . . Small wonder then that [some] wild rumors of large-scale graft and embezzlement circulated during the statue's construction. Immediately after the dedication, charges were brought against Phidias [by Pericles's political opponents], and vigorous efforts were made to involve Pericles himself in the scandal. . . . Phidias reportedly detached and weighed the gold plates to prove his innocence, but feelings were running so high that he judged it advisable to leave town in some haste rather than stand trial. He went to Olympia . . . where, probably in 433 [B.C.], the sculptor died without ever having returned to Athens.

Peter Green. *The Parthenon*. New York: Newsweek Book Division, 1981, p. 82.

Greek figures fighting the Amazons look exactly like himself and his friend Pericles. Plutarch wrote:

> The fame of Phidias's works still served to arouse jealousy against him, especially because in the relief of the battle of the Amazons, which is represented on the shield of the goddess, he carved a figure representing himself as a bald old man lifting up a stone with both hands, and also because he introduced a particularly fine likeness of Pericles fighting an Amazon. The position of the hand, which holds a spear in front of Pericles' face, seems to have been ingeniously contrived to conceal the resemblance, but it can still be seen quite plainly from either side.[38]

Ivory Skin, Golden Robes

The enormous statue of Athena was made of a core wooden framework covered in ivory for her skin and large sheets of pure gold for her clothing, helmet, and shield. To make the gold sheets required, Phidias and his assistants had to create a full-sized clay model of each section of the figure. Once the clay had been shaped to the master's satisfaction, the assistants made negative plaster molds of each section. They then laid thin sheets of gold into these hollow molds and with wooden mallets beat the soft metal until it conformed to the mold's outlines. Finally, the gold sheets were removed from the molds and attached to the huge wooden framework by means of metal clamps and wooden dowels. According to ancient accounts, about 2,500 pounds (1,134kg) of gold was used in all.

Phidias employed the same methods to create another colossal cult image—the so-called Olympian Zeus. It portrayed the leader of the gods sitting on a throne in the cella of the Temple of Zeus at Olympia, an artwork later designated one of the Seven Wonders of the Ancient World. As in the case of the *Athena Parthenos*, the monumental Zeus has not survived. But once again Pausanias supplied an eyewitness account, saying:

The god is sitting on a throne. He is made of gold and ivory. There is a wreath in his head like twigs and leaves of olive. In his right hand he is holding a [figure of the goddess] Victory of gold and ivory with a ribbon and a wreath on her head. In the god's left hand is a staff in blossom with every kind of precious metal, and the bird perching on his staff is Zeus's eagle [one of his symbols]. The sandals are gold and so is his cloak, and the cloak is inlaid with animals and flowering lilies. The throne is finely worked with gold and gems, and with ebony and with ivory. Upon it, moreover, are painted figures and sculpted images. . . . [Some people] say even that the god himself bore witness to the art of Phidias. When the statue was completely finished, Phidias prayed to the god to make a sign if the work pleased him, and immediately a flash of lightning struck the pavement at the place where the bronze urn was still standing in my time.[39]

The Culmination of Realism

All of Phidias's giant statues contained large amounts of detail because he strove to make these images look as lifelike as possible. This is not surprising, since the evolution of Greek sculpture over the centuries had witnessed an ongoing trend toward realism. This movement continued for the remainder of classical times and reached its culmination in the subsequent Hellenistic age.

In the Classical era, sculptors had most often chosen gods, heroes, and other mythical or supernatural beings for subjects, which they typically showed in idealized situations and poses. In contrast, in the Hellenistic Age sculptors and other artists "produced realistic renderings of a cross section of the population," Sarah B. Pomeroy writes. Indeed, they quite often focused "on the individual as special and unique."[40] This was because society in the new era placed a larger emphasis on the individual person and his or her desires, needs, and personal happiness.

This sculptural cross section of humanity was most often depicted in small, inexpensive figurines made of terra-cotta (baked clay), which sculptors turned out by the thousands in Hellenistic times. "The figurines portrayed people of all ages," Pomeroy continues, "every social status, and a range of ethnicities, including chubby children; stooped, stout, and wrinkled elderly people; elegant and graceful society women; and members of the lower classes."[41]

Although there was a distinct upsurge in realistic portrayals of ordinary people in Hellenistic sculpture, the new age still pursued the artistic depiction of ideal heroes and gods that had been so popular in classical times. In fact, Hellenistic sculptors, and the era's artists in general, often tested the limits of realism in art. When possible, they attempted to endow their carved figures with new heights of emotion and drama.

The most striking example of this trend was the huge sculpted frieze that wound around the base of the great Altar of Zeus at Pergamum. That extraordinary artwork included seventy-five sculpted figures representing the gods and giants

During the Hellenistic period sculptors tested the limits of realism in art. The most striking example of this trend is found in the seventy-five figures in the huge frieze that wound around the base of the Altar of Zeus in Pergamum.

in the midst of the Gigantomachy, their faces contorted in astonishing displays of anger, fear, frustration, and agony. "The torsos of both gods and giants are treated like rugged landscapes in themselves," one modern expert remarks. "The combat immediately involves the viewer on approach, by appearing to spill off the edge of the [sculpted panel] and onto the altar steps."[42] This is not meant in the symbolic or figurative sense. Some of the limbs of the fighting figures actually extend outward from the frieze and rest on the nearest steps. This achievement marked the culmination of realism in Greek sculpture. It was a larger-than-life approach that inspired the Romans and centuries later the artists of the Renaissance to employ striking theatrical styles of their own.

5

The Pioneers of Greek Painting

Like Greek sculpture, Greek painting underwent an evolution in which its practitioners at first produced rudimentary, sketchy work and over time strove increasingly to achieve visual realism. The only paintings known to have existed in the Dark Age were those on the outer surfaces of cups, vases, and other pottery items. Between about 1050 and 900 B.C. (called the Protogeometric period of Greek art), such painting consisted strictly of whirls, zigzags, cross-hatching, and other simplistic linear designs. Not until the period spanning 900 to 700 B.C. (the Geometric period of Greek art) did artists attempt to depict animals and human figures on pottery. Yet these were only crude silhouettes with little or no detail.

The beginnings in Greece of what people today would recognize as true paintings—artistic renderings in color on surfaces other than pottery—took place in the Archaic Age. Extremely few samples of these works have survived. One, found at Pitsa (near Corinth), done on a wooden plaque, shows a religious procession in which some adults and children are about to sacrifice a sheep. The figures are rendered in elegant line drawings with solid colors added—flesh tones for skin and red and blue for clothing. But detail, shading, perspective (to indicate varying distance), and other aspects of realism are lacking.

In fact, it was not until well into the Classical Age that these elements of painting technique appeared, and not all at once. According to surviving ancient sources, they were introduced one at a time, each by a popular painter of his day, whose innovation was immediately adopted by his contemporaries. In this way, these painting pioneers moved the craft forward, ever closer to what painters viewed as the ideal. This was to make painted objects look as realistic as their counterparts in the natural world.

In the late Classical and early Hellenistic periods, this ambitious goal was finally achieved. Illustrating it was a charming fable passed on by Pliny the Elder in which two leading painters, Zeuxis (ZOOK-sis) and Parrhasios (pa-RAY-shi-us), had a contest to see which could more convincingly fool the eye. Zeuxis boasted he had painted some grapes that looked so real they had attracted birds. Parrhasios countered that he

The Pitsa tablet is a rare example of painting from the Archaic Age.

could do a painting of an object that would fool not only animals but also humans, and he invited his opponent to his house for a demonstration. When Zeuxis arrived, he asked to see the painting, and Parrhasios told him to look behind a curtain. But when Zeuxis went to draw back the curtain, he found it was not a real curtain but only a painting of a curtain! Realizing that he had been fooled, he conceded the contest to Parrhasios.

Polygnotus, the "Old Master"

Zeuxis and Parrhasios lived in the late 400s and early 300s B.C. Their work and success were made possible in part by several earlier painting pioneers, among them the gifted and famous Polygnotus (pa-lig-NOH-tis). Sometimes called the "Old Master" of Greek painting, he was born on the northern Aegean island of Thasos but as a young man moved to Athens. There he was active from about 480 to 450 B.C., when Pericles and Phidias were young men. About Polygnotus, University of Louisville scholar Robert B. Kebric writes:

> Innovative, brash, confident in his skills, Polygnotus spent much of his adult life in Athens and was the first known artistic advisor to an Athenian politician—Cimon, who he recognized as his patron. Undoubtedly, it was Cimon's influence that helped the artist obtain Athenian citizenship, an honor not frequently bestowed on foreigners, but it was Polygnotus's own virtues . . . that attracted the affections of Cimon's free-spirited sister, Elpinice, who became his lover and model.[43]

Of Polygnotus's many works, the best known was a wall painting, or mural, titled *The Capture of Troy*, which was long on display at Delphi. No traces of it remain. In fact, none of the murals and other major paintings from Classical times have survived. The only means of determining what they looked like are surviving ancient literary accounts. Of those that describe *The Capture of Troy*, that of Pausanias says that it contained a number of important mythical figures from the Trojan War. They include Helen, the Spartan queen whose abduction by Troy's

Based upon a Polygnotus painting, this Greek red-figure plate depicts Achilles slaying the Amazon Penthisilea. The work shows the artist's innovations in creating depth and perspective.

Prince Paris sparked the conflict; her husband, King Menelaus (men-uh-LAY-us); Diomedes (dy-uh-MEE-deez), ruler of another Greek kingdom, Argos; Troy's king, Priam; and other characters that were well known to the average ancient Greek but are fairly obscure today. The painting, Pausanias said,

> shows the fall of Troy and the Greeks sailing away. Menelaus's men are getting ready for the voyage [back to Greece at the war's end]. There is a painting of the ship with a mixture of men and boys among the sailors, and

the ship's steersman, Phrontis, standing amidships holding two poles. . . . [Some men] are taking down Menelaus's tent not far from the ship. [The maiden] Briseis is standing with Diomedes above her and Iphis in front of them as if they are all gazing at Helen's beauty. Helen herself is standing with Eurybates near her, [and] above Helen sits a man wrapped in a purple cloak, extremely melancholy. You would know it was Priam's son Helenus even before you read the inscription.[44]

This and other paintings by Polygnotus utilized an important innovation attributed to him. This was the method of

PAUSON AND THE HORSE

Very little is known about the life and works of the late-fifth-century-B.C. Athenian painter Pauson. The comic playwright Aristophanes mentions him briefly in three of his plays. These references suggest that the painter was known for depicting subjects relating to the lower classes, perhaps including practices and character types that most Greeks viewed as seedy or immoral. Also, an amusing story about Pauson, one that if true provides some revealing commentary on his character, has survived. According to the later Greek writer Lucian of Samosata:

Pauson the painter was commissioned to do a horse rolling [on its back]. He painted one galloping in a cloud of dust. As he was at work upon it, his patron [customer] came in, and complained that this was not what he had ordered. Pauson just turned the picture upside down and told his man to hold it so for inspection. There was the horse rolling on its back, [he told the man].

Lucian. *Demosthenes: An Encomium*. Translated by H.W. Fowler. Internet Sacred Text Archive. www.sacred-texts.com/cla/luc/wl4/wl429.htm.

placing his figures at different levels across the painting in order to convey a feeling of depth, since no one yet knew how to show true perspective. (In drawing and painting, perspective is the technique of showing, on paper or another flat surface, people and objects getting smaller as their distance from the observer increases, just as perceived by the eye in real life.) Kebric explains that to represent, or symbolize, this effect, Polygnotus placed

> individuals, or groups of individuals, on different levels, scattering them about at various points in space, instead of confining them to a single ground line as had previously been done. Landscape figures such as trees and rocks gave an additional feeling of depth. Also, an emotional quality appears to have characterized his work, with figures reacting to what has just happened or what is about to happen.[45]

Perspective and Shading

Not long after Polygnotus's heyday, his younger contemporary, Agatharchus (ag-uh-THAR-kis), introduced a set of rules for showing true perspective, called *scenographia* (scene painting) in Greek art. The first major use of the technique appears to have been in scenic background paintings for stage shows sometime in the late fifth century B.C. According to Vitruvius:

> Agatharchus, at Athens, when [the noted playwright] Aeschylus was presenting a tragedy, was in control of the stage and . . . show[ed] how, if a fixed center [the vanishing point] is taken for the outward glance of the eyes and the projection of the radii [converging lines of sight], we must follow these lines in accordance with a natural law, such that . . . uncertain images may give the appearance of buildings in the scenery of the stage, and how what is figured upon vertical and plane surfaces can seem to recede in one part [of the painting] and project [outward] in another.[46]

One classical painter who was almost certainly influenced by Polygnotus and Agatharchus was Panainos (puh-NYE-nos). The latter worked closely with his brother, the great sculptor Phidias. Panainos not only worked on the giant Zeus at Olympia, but also produced several large murals that adorned other structures at that great athletic center. One showed the mythical character Atlas holding up the heavens, with the legendary strongman Heracles (the Roman Hercules) about to relieve him of the burden. Also, Pausanias described a painting by Panainos that depicted Heracles killing the vicious Nemean Lion, one of the well-known Twelve Labors performed by that famous hero.

Still another artistic advance attributed to Greek artists was the perfection of the technique of shading, or *sciagraphia*. Shading is the use of contouring, that is, increasing or decreasing lightness or darkness on painted bodies or objects to give the illusion of three dimensions. The ancient sources claimed that the Athenian painter Apollodorus (a-pa-luh-DOR-us) was responsible for this major breakthrough. His dates remain uncertain, but it seems likely he was active in the late fifth century B.C., making him a contemporary of Agatharchus and Panainos. Later Greek painters incorporated and improved on Apollodorus's methods of shading, making their subjects look astonishingly realistic.

The Great Age: Zeuxis

Indeed, because of such advances, the period that followed these pioneers—the early fourth century B.C.—later became known as the great age of Greek painting. In those years, Zeuxis built an enormous reputation for his painting skills and became a wealthy man thanks to the many commissions he received from the rich and famous of various city-states. The noted first-century-B.C. Roman writer and orator Cicero wrote that a committee of citizens from the Greek city of Crotona desired to commission a painting to adorn a local temple and for that project

> hired Zeuxis of Heraclea at a vast price, who was at that time considered to be far superior to all other painters,

The brother of the great sculptor Phidias, Panainos, was a well-known Athenian painter in the late fifth century B.C. Almost nothing is known about Panainos's personal life. But ancient authors described some of his painting projects. The Roman scholar Pliny the Elder, for example, said he created (with the aid of two other artists) a large painted mural depicting the famous Battle of Marathon, fought between the Greeks and Persians in 490 B.C. Included in the work, Pliny claimed, were portraits of the major Greek heroes of the battle. The second-century-A.D. Greek traveler Pausanias saw the painting and told how "in the heart of the battle the barbarians [Persians] are in flight, pushing each other into the marsh, and the painting ends with the . . . Greeks slaughtering barbarians as they jump into [their ships]."[1] The most famous project Panainos worked on was the majestic statue of Olympian Zeus, on which he collaborated with his brother. According to the first-century-B.C. Greek writer Strabo, "Panainos the painter, Phidias's own brother and his coworker, was a great help to him in the decoration of the statue, especially the drapery [of the god's tunic], with colors. There are a good number of quite marvelous paintings on display around the sanctuary which are the work of that artist."[2]

1. Pausanias. *Guide to Greece*. Vol. 1. Translated by Peter Levi. New York: Penguin, 1971, pp. 45–46.
2. Strabo. *Geography*. Quoted in J.J. Pollitt, ed. and trans. *The Art of Ancient Greece: Sources and Documents*. New York: Cambridge University Press, 1990, pp. 61–62.

None of Panainos's paintings have survived, although the artist also worked with his brother on the statue of Olympian Zeus.

and employed him in that business. . . . In order that one of his [works] might contain the preeminent beauty of the female form, he said that he wished to paint a likeness of Helen [of Troy, who was known for her great beauty]. And the men of Crotona, who had frequently heard that he exceeded all other men in painting women, were very glad to hear this, for they thought that if he took the greatest pains in that class of work in which he had the greatest skill, he would leave them a most noble work in that temple.[47]

Like those of most other Greek masters, Zeuxis's paintings are all lost. But the second-century-A.D. Greek writer Lucian of Samosata described one of that painter's finest murals, which depicted some centaurs (SEN-tawrs), mythical beings having the upper body of a human and the lower body of a horse. Lucian's extraordinary account is also valuable for two other reasons. First, it mentions one of the common ways that original Greek artworks were destroyed over the years; second, it makes the point that it was common for later generations to make copies of the originals—paintings, statues, and other works—for commercial purposes, a practice still widespread today. Lucian said:

One of these daring pieces by [Zeuxis] represented a female Centaur nursing a pair of infant Centaur twins. There is a copy of the picture now at Athens, taken exactly from the original. The latter is said to have been put on a ship, bound for Italy with the rest of [the Roman general] Sulla's art treasures [stolen from Greece], and to have been lost with them by the sinking of the ship. . . . The picture of the picture I have seen, and the best word-picture I can manage of that I [will] now give you. . . . On fresh green [grass] appears the mother Centaur, the whole equine part of her stretched on the ground, her hoofs extended backwards; the human part is slightly raised on the elbows. The fore feet are not extended like the others. . . . One of them is bent as in the act of kneeling, with the hoof tucked in, while the other is beginning to straighten and take a hold on the ground—the action of a horse rising. Of the cubs she is holding, one is in her arms suckling in the human fashion, while the other is drawing at the mare's [nipple] like a foal. In the upper part of the picture, as on higher ground, is a Centaur who is clearly the husband of the nursing mother. He leans over laughing, visible only down to the middle of his horse body. He holds a lion [cub] aloft in his right hand, terrifying the youngsters with it in sport. . . . What strikes me especially about Zeuxis is the manifold [diverse] scope which he has found for his extraordinary skill in a single [painting]. You have in the husband a truly terrible savage creature. . . . Even in his merry mood, [he is] brutal, uncivilized, [and] wild. In contrast with him, the animal half of the female is lovely [and her] human upper half is also most beautiful.[48]

This nineteenth-century painting depicts the artist Zeuxis using five models to aid him in reproducing the beauty of Helen of Troy. Her likeness appeared on a mural he painted in Crotona in the early fourth century B.C.

The Great Age: Apelles

The ancient writers, including Pliny the Elder, all agreed that although Zeuxis was a great painter, there was a Greek who was even greater. He was Apelles (uh-PEL-eez) of Kos, who was active in the late fourth century B.C., the early years of the Hellenistic Age. Because of his tremendous talent and skills, Apelles was always in huge demand. Moreover, he painted portraits of and got to know many of the rulers and major military generals of his day. For a while he was a court painter in Macedonia, where he did portraits of the brilliant military innovator King Philip II and his renowned son, Alexander III (later called "the Great"). One of Apelles's most acclaimed works was a picture of Alexander holding a thunderbolt.

Jacques-Louis David's 1814 painting *Apelles and Pancaste* depicts Apelles painting Pancaste, Alexander the Great's mistress, in the nude.

Alexander greatly admired the painter and was said to have rewarded him in an unusual way. According to Pliny:

> The king was particularly fond of Pancaste, one of his mistresses, and, out of admiration for her physical beauty, he commissioned Apelles to paint her in the nude. When Alexander realized that Apelles had fallen in love with his subject, he gave Pancaste to the artist. . . . Some authorities think that she was the model for [Apelles' highly regarded work] *Aphrodite Rising from the Foam.*[49]

Another famous painting by Apelles was a large-scale likeness of one of Alexander's most colorful and infamous generals, Antigonus the One-Eyed (who later, after his boss's death, vied with others for control of the vast empire Alexander had amassed). This commission displayed Apelles's diplomacy and cleverness, as recalled by Pliny: "Apelles also painted a portrait of King Antigonus, who had lost his eye. He was the first artist to devise a way of hiding the defect. He drew the portrait in three-quarters view, so that the missing eye would not appear in the picture, and he showed only that part of the king's face that he could present intact."[50]

One of Apelles' greatest works was said by some ancient sources to be a large depiction of a battle between Alexander and Persia's King Darius III. Like other major ancient Greek paintings, it was lost over the years. But there is a chance it may have survived indirectly in a copy done in mosaics well after its creator's death. In the nineteenth century, archaeologists found the work, which they dubbed the "Alexander Mosaic," in the House of the Faun in the Roman town of Pompeii (pom-PAY), which was buried in a volcanic eruption in A.D. 79. The house's owner had commissioned a Greek artist to complete the mosaic. Supposedly, that artist used Apelles's famous painting as the model. If this story is true, the likeness of Alexander in the mosaic is likely fairly accurate, because Apelles knew him well.[51]

Apelles was so masterly and celebrated that his reputation survived him by many centuries. During Europe's Renaissance,

"So Great Was Her Talent"

Ancient Greek society was patriarchal, or male-dominated. So the vast majority of artists in Greece, including painters, were men. Nevertheless, a handful of women managed to learn the painting trade and sell their works. This happened most often when a male painter had no sons to carry on his trade and taught what he knew to his daughter. This may have been the case with Timarete, daughter of the Athenian painter Micon. Pliny the Elder mentioned her along with other female painters, saying that she created a well-known likeness of the goddess Artemis. Pliny added:

Irene, daughter and student of [the dramatist] Cratinus, painted a girl at Eleusis, a [portrait of the nymph] Calypso, the old juggler Theodorus, and the dancer Alcisthenes. [Also] Iaia of Cyzicus, who never married, worked in Rome [in the early first century B.C.]. She painted women most frequently, including a panel picture of an old woman in Naples, and even a self-portrait for which she used a mirror. No one's hand was quicker to paint a picture than hers. So great was her talent that her prices far exceeded those of the most celebrated [male] painters of her day.

Pliny the Elder. *Natural History*. Quoted in Mary R. Lefkowitz and Maureen B. Fant, eds. *Women's Life in Greece and Rome: A Source Book in Translation*. Baltimore: Johns Hopkins University Press, 1992, pp. 216–217.

the grand outburst of great artworks spanning the fourteenth through sixteenth centuries, several painters acknowledged their debt to him and attempted to equal his genius. Among these admirers was the great Italian artist Sandro Botticelli. Later still, in the eighteenth century, another great Italian painter, Giovanni Battista Tiepolo, painted a magnificent canvas showing Alexander sitting for a portrait in Apelles's studio.

Although Apelles was tremendously talented, his achievements would not have been possible without the techniques and traditions established by previous Greek painters. So the fact that Renaissance and early modern painters were profoundly inspired by him is a testament to the crucial role that ancient Greek painting played in the formative stages of Western art.

6

Pottery, Metalwork, and Other Crafts

Examples of the major arts of architecture, sculpture, and painting abounded in ancient Greece. They were the ones on the biggest scale—the most visible to large numbers of people at any given moment. The Greeks also excelled at a number of smaller-scale arts, however. Potters, for instance, turned out all manner of beautiful vases, drinking cups, pitchers, kraters (or craters, large containers for mixing wine and water), burial urns, oil flasks, amphorae (storage jars), and many more. Many were produced for commercial purposes. But of these, most were not cheap, mediocre goods, as are so many of today's commercial products. Rather, the vast majority of Greek pots were carefully and finely made, and a fairly high proportion can be categorized as nothing less than works of art. The same can be said for much of the metalwork, jewelry, and glasswork turned out by Greek artisans.

Pre-classical Greek Ceramics

The first of these fine crafts, and indeed the earliest known artwork of any kind in Greece, was pottery, or ceramics. In fact, pottery was made during the Dark Age, although most high-quality examples did not appear until the second half of that period. The first distinct Dark Age style, now referred to

A neck-handled amphora from the Protogeometric period of the Greek Dark Age shows two designs of concentric circles, characteristic of the period's style.

as Protogeometric, appeared about 1050 B.C. The chief center of production was at first Athens, one of the few Greek sites that had not been devastated and abandoned at the close of the Bronze Age. Over time the style spread to other parts of Greece. These items were made in a limited number of shapes, including several distinct versions of amphorae, and were decorated mostly with brown or black designs painted on a light

A black-figure bowl and stand, signed by Sophilos. The artist pioneered the "black figure" style, which featured people, animals, and objects depicted in black on a reddish-brown clay surface.

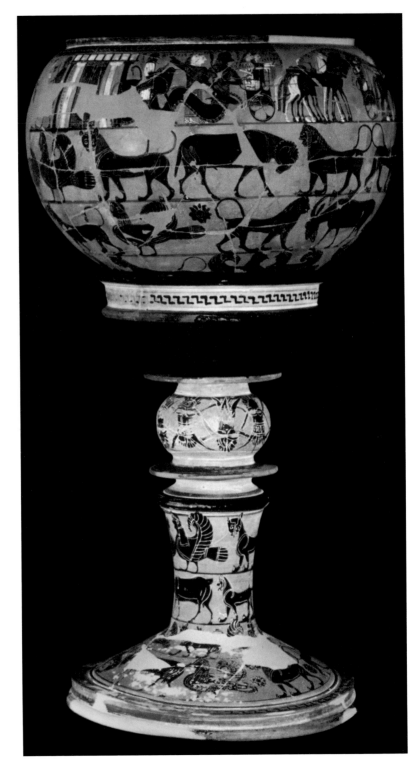

clay background. The designs were repetitive and included half circles, cross-hatching, and the right-angled pattern that later came to be called the meander, or Greek key.

In the Geometric period that began about 900 B.C., the variety of shapes of ceramic items increased. Also, it was common for a potter to cover an item with black glaze and use a light-on-dark scheme of decoration. Typical among geometric designs were triangles, squares, and zigzags, along with cross-hatching and the meander. Toward the end of the period (in the 700s B.C.), the black glaze became less and less prominent, giving way to bands of figures painted onto a brownish buff or yellowish surface. Increasingly, the figures were likenesses of living things, including horses, birds, deer, and humans. One of the finest surviving examples of late Geometric pottery is the so-called Dyplon Amphora (because it was found near Athens's Dyplon Gate), dated to about 750 B.C. David Sacks describes it, saying:

> Amid bands of meanders and diamond shapes, a panel shows triangular-torsoed stick figures in postures of mourning around a skirted figure on a bier [a stand holding a corpse]. Appropriately, the five-foot-tall vase was deposited as an offering [to the gods] in an aristocratic tomb. The vase's artist, named the "Dyplon painter" by scholars, is considered to be the first recognizably individual Greek artist.[52]

Greek ceramics continued to evolve, in part because of cultural influences gained in expanding trade with foreign peoples, especially in the Middle East. By about 730 or 720 B.C., Eastern influences had brought about a style (and art period) that modern experts dubbed "Orientalizing." Some new shapes appeared, most notably the *aryballos*, a small, round perfume container with a narrow mouth. The first major center for both the new style and production of the *aryballos* was Corinth, which in the 600s B.C. underwent considerable growth and became known as a commercial and arts hub. Common Orientalist-painted motifs included plant leaves and stems, the dot rosette (a central dot encircled by other dots), and prominent, often dramatic depictions of animals and people.

In the 500s B.C., the final century before the start of the Classical Age, two major new pottery styles originated in Athens, which eventually came to surpass Corinth as an arts center. The first of these styles was called "black figure" because figures of people, animals, and objects were painted in black onto the natural reddish-brown clay surface. After the pot was baked, the potter-artist employed a pointed tool to etch extra details into the figures.

Among the black-figure pioneers was the Athenian Sophilos, the first known potter who signed his work. Another major black-figure potter became popular from about 550 to 525 B.C. His real name remains unknown, so archaeologists and historians refer to him as the "Amasis Painter" (after the Athenian who owned the building in which he worked).

Classical Greek Pottery

The second new Athenian pottery style appeared in about 520 B.C. and remained popular in the first half of the Classical Age. It was called "red figure" because it depicted human and animal figures in the baked pot's natural reddish-brown tone against a black background. This allowed the potter to strive for more realistic details, which he added with a brush. One of the many talented red-figure potters, called the "Berlin Painter" by modern experts, was known for his realistic renderings of human limbs and muscles. His colleague, the "Brygos Painter," became famous for painting detailed scenes on the bottoms of drinking cups. Other classical artists who excelled in the red-figure technique were the Niobid Painter, the Achilles Painter, and the Meidias Painter.

Although red-figure pottery continued to be made in the late fifth century B.C., other styles of pottery decoration became popular as well. One, known as the "white-ground" method, featured figures painted in thin, dark lines against a white background. The most common ceramic item in this new style was the lekythos, a tall, slender container frequently (though not exclusively) used to hold liquids intended as funeral offerings.

To make a lekythos, krater, vase, or other elegant ceramic piece, a classical Greek potter employed most of the same steps as earlier practitioners of his art. He took some wet clay, called *ceramos* (from which the term *ceramic* derives) and placed it on his potter's wheel. The wheel spun around on a vertical spindle that he either turned by hand himself or had an assistant turn.

After modeling the clay into the desired shape, the potter put it outside in the sun to dry. Then he painted it and/or added one or more glazes, after which he placed it in a wood-burning kiln. "The pots were stacked inverted [upside-down] within an oval or circular chamber," a modern expert explains. "A stokehole or stoking tunnel was on one side, and the hot

An Attic red-figure cup by the Brygos Painter depicts a scene from the Trojan War. In the "red-figure" style, objects appeared in the natural reddish-brown color of baked clay and were set off against a black background.

gases rose from the fire around the pots and out a vent at the top of the kiln."[53] The result was an attractive, sometimes elegant, and always highly durable ceramic object that if safely stored was capable of lasting for many centuries. Indeed, more than a few ancient Greek pottery items on display in museums today look like they were created only a year or two ago.

Metalworking Methods

The classical Greeks' traditions in the art of metalwork went back to the late Dark Age, making them almost as old as their pottery-making traditions. Most of their metal objects, including the decorative ones, were fashioned from a few basic metals. They included copper, bronze (copper plus tin), iron, lead, gold, silver, and electrum (gold plus silver). From the 500s B.C. on, Thomas Craven wrote,

> metalwork was almost as popular as monumental art [like architecture and sculpture]. Every bronze appliance was graced with style and distinction. Mirrors polished on one side to serve as reflectors, and engraved on the other to beguile [charm] the tired eye, were staples in the markets, in company with a long list of common articles, such as [oil] lamps, vases, drinking goblets, and candlesticks, all decorated [beautifully].[54]

To make a candlestick or other metal item, the Greeks most often began with ores, mixtures of rock and metal. Working usually right at the mining site, they melted broken pieces of ore in fires or furnaces, producing a thick liquid version of copper, silver, or another metal. They then poured the softened metal into molds to make ingots, or bars, which they sent off to artisans in various cities.

Having received one or more ingots, an artisan employed one of various traditional methods to create the desired metal object or objects. The simplest involved melting down the ingot and pouring the softened metal into a hand-carved, hollow stone mold. After the metal had cooled and solidified, the artisan removed it from the mold and used a file or another tool to remove any imperfections in its surface.

TRIPODS AND OTHER BRONZE OBJECTS

Greek metalworkers made bronze objects for a wide array of uses, as explained here by Metropolitan Museum of Art scholar Amy Sowder.

Bronze vessels were made in a wide range of shapes over a long period of time. Many of the earliest vessels, dating to the ninth and eighth centuries B.C., were tripods, which are three-legged stands that supported large cauldrons. Sometimes the two parts were made together in one piece. The cauldrons were originally used as cooking pots, but the tripods also were given as prizes for winners in athletic contests. The edges of the cauldrons and stands could be decorated with protomes (foreparts) of animals or mythical creatures. Powerful animals such as lions and horses appear frequently. The griffin—a fantastic beast with the body of a lion and the head of an eagle—and the sphinx—with a feline [catlike] body and a human head—were favorite motifs. Water jars (hydriai) seem to have been a preferred shape in bronze. The characteristic shape of a hydria is well suited to its function, with a narrow neck for preventing spills, a rounded belly for holding water, a vertical handle for pouring, and two lateral handles for lifting. A long series of hydriai survive, spanning the Archaic, Classical, and Hellenistic periods.

Amy Sowder. "Ancient Greek Bronze Vessels." Metropolitan Museum of Art. www.metmuseum.org/toah/hd/agbv/hd_agbv.htm.

This tripod cauldron from the eighth century B.C. is an example of early Greek metalworking.

A more complicated approach was called the "lost-wax" method. In it, the artisan first created a wax model of a candlestick or other object he wanted to render in metal form. Then he coated the wax with clay. When the clay dried and became stiff, he melted away the wax, leaving its detailed impression on the clay's inner surface. Into this hollow clay mold he poured softened metal and allowed it to cool and solidify. In the final step, the artisan removed the clay, revealing the finished candlestick or other item.

To create large, hollow bronze objects, such as statues or busts, the artisan might use a third method, called hollow casting. He began by making a roughly shaped clay core and applying a thick layer of wax to it. Then he carefully modeled the wax to look like the desired object. Next he covered the wax with a layer of wet clay and heated it all in an oven. The heat caused the clay layers to harden but melted the wax, leaving behind hollow spaces conforming to the shape and details of the original wax model. Finally, the artisan poured softened metal into the hollow spaces, and when the metal cooled and hardened, he peeled away the clay, exposing the finished statue or other object.

Jewelry Making

Another combination of craft and art in which Greek artisans used metals, especially bronze, gold, silver, and electrum, was jewelry making. Also commonly used by jewelers were semiprecious stones, such as amethyst, agate, rock crystal, garnet, and chalcedony. In addition, pearls and glass were frequently employed in Greek jewelry making.

Whatever materials were used, jewelry was extremely popular in the Greek lands. In the Classical and Hellenistic eras, women who could afford it wore elegant necklaces, but even less expensive necklaces and other examples of costume jewelry were well made and attractive. In addition to necklaces, common jewelry pieces worn by women included rings, bracelets, brooches (mostly for fastening clothes), earrings, anklets, headbands, and armbands. Men also wore rings. (The famous Athenian scholar and philosopher Aristotle wore several rings at one time.)

To make a ring, say of gold, a jeweler first obtained a sheet of gold that had been hammered until it was very thin. (Some jewelers may have made such sheets themselves.) The next step was to slice the gold, a relatively soft metal, into thin strips. These could then be cut into smaller pieces of the desired lengths, some of which were suitable for ring making. The jeweler twisted such a strip into a circular shape and heated the ends to merge them and close the circle. The ring might be left plain or it might be further decorated by carving it or inlaying it with colorful stones or other eye-catching items.

These exquisite gold earrings from the third century B.C. have discs mounted on top of Victory figures playing the game knucklebones, with dolls and females dancers to the sides.

Greek Glass

Among those other items that were sometimes worked into rings, bracelets, and other kinds of jewelry was glass. The ancient Greeks utilized two principal types of glass. One was the transparent or semitransparent variety, which was manufactured using three different techniques. In the first the glassmaker collected some sand and heated it at a high temperature until it melted into liquid glass. Using a metal rod to keep his hands from burning, he then dipped a pottery core into the hot liquid. The latter stuck to the core, forming a layer that cooled and hardened. (The artisan might add two or more additional layers, depending on the thickness he desired.) Next the glassmaker inserted a pointed tool through an opening in the object and broke up the pottery core. Carefully, he shook the object, causing the pieces of the core to fall out, leaving behind a glass shell.

This Hellenistic faience blue glass bowl is from the second century B.C.

In the second method, called "cold cutting," the artisan sliced a heated, semisoft glass bar into one or more desired shapes and allowed the objects to cool and harden. The third technique was known as "molding." In it, the glassmaker poured liquid or semisoft glass into a wooden mold, allowed it to cool, and removed the finished object from the mold.

The second main type of glass in Greece was faience. It consisted of crushed quartz or sand that the artisan converted into a paste and covered with colored glazes. The two most popular colors for glazes were blue and green, although all the other colors were available as well. Among the more common items made from faience were bowls, vases, wine jugs, amulets, jewelry beads, pendants, and figurines.

Some faience items were made in Greece, while others were imported from Egypt, Syria (an important glass-making center), and elsewhere. It is sometimes difficult for archaeologists to determine which ones were domestically made and which were imported. More certain is that most faience was expensive, so it long remained a luxury item. This situation changed significantly, however, following the invention of glassblowing in Syria in the first century B.C. With that new, revolutionary method, a number of glass products came to be mass-produced. That brought down their price. Still, some glass items remained costly specialty items, particularly those that achieved the clearest transparency and those that were intricately decorated with thin strips of metal or colored glasses.

Good-bye to Greek Art?

Whether it was glass, ceramics, sculpture, or some other artistic genre, historians and other modern experts never tire of pointing out the special qualities of the ancient Greek arts and the gifted individuals who created them. They emphasize that architecture, sculpture, painting, and other arts in the Western world today were deeply influenced by the artistic achievements of the Renaissance and the centuries that immediately followed it. In turn, many Renaissance artists were profoundly influenced by the ancient Greek arts.

ALEXANDER'S SPLENDID FUNERAL CARRIAGE

Among the finest artworks created in the ancient Greek lands were those that combined several artistic disciplines in a single object. A splendid example of this multigenre approach was the funeral carriage made in 323 B.C. to carry the body of Alexander the Great from Babylon (where he had died) back to Macedonia. (On the way, it was hijacked by one of his generals, Ptolemy, and taken to Egypt.) According to the first-century-B.C. Greek historian Diodorus Siculus, the carriage featured a combination of fine metalworking and wood-working, jeweled inlays, sculpted and painted panels, and fabric embroidered with gold strands. His description says in part:

On the top of the casket a gold cover was placed, fitting it exactly, [and] on top of this was placed a splendid purple robe, embroidered with gold, beside which they placed [his] armor. [Above the casket, the carriage had] a vaulted gold roof decorated with scales studded with jewels. . . . Beneath the roof and running around the whole work was a gold cornice [ornate molding], with goat-stag protomes [depictions of animals] done in high relief, from which gold rings [hung]. . . . At the corners of the vault on each side there was a gold [statue of the goddess] Nike bearing a trophy. [The carriage also held paintings, one] representing a chariot with embossed decoration and in it was seated Alexander, holding a splendid scepter in his hands.

Diodorus Siculus. *Library of History.* Quoted in J.J. Pollitt, ed. and trans. *The Art of Ancient Greece: Sources and Documents.* New York: Cambridge University Press, 1990, p. 218.

As for what made the Greek arts so exceptional, experts sometimes point to the mental attitudes of the artists themselves. They also cite the social and political climate in which those talented individuals worked. Among others, Thomas Craven held that the Greeks were the only known people in history who "put art above all other pursuits." Moreover, he said, the Greek artist "was an absolutely free agent," whose "spirit and imagination were never enslaved."[55]

Indeed, unlike their modern counterparts, Greek artists were often encouraged through both financial and moral support by their governments and fellow citizens. A unique mix of patriotic, social, and religious influences urged them to be creative and to produce works of quality that would benefit society, please the gods, and stand the test of time. In this respect, the Greek artist "was his own master," Craven said. As a result, "the best of Greek art is exalted and pure and clean, never tainted by the indecent, the coarse, the cheap, or the mercenary, never stooping to the sensational, the [meaningless], and the [insincere]. We can never say good-bye to the Greeks as artists."[56]

Notes

Introduction: The First Westerners

1. Thomas Craven. *The Pocket Book of Greek Art.* New York: Pocket Books, 1950, pp. 6, 17.
2. Edith Hamilton. *The Greek Way.* New York: Norton, 1993, pp. 16, 25.
3. C.M. Bowra. *Classical Greece.* New York: Time-Life, 1977, p. 14.
4. Bowra. *Classical Greece*, p. 14.
5. Nigel Spivey. *Greek Art.* London: Phaidon, 1997, pp. 382–384.

Chapter 1: The Art of Greece's Bronze Age

6. Diodorus Siculus. *Library of History.* Quoted in J.J. Pollitt, ed. and trans. *The Art of Ancient Greece: Sources and Documents.* New York: Cambridge University Press, 1990, p. 12.
7. Sarah B. Pomeroy et al. *Ancient Greece: A Political, Social, and Cultural History.* New York: Oxford University Press, 2007, p. 15.
8. Nanno Marinatos. *Art and Religion in Thera: Reconstructing a Bronze Age City.* Athens: D. and I. Mathioulakis, 1984, p. 33.
9. Chester G. Starr. *A History of the Ancient World.* New York: Oxford University Press, 1991, p. 107.
10. Maitland A. Edey. *Lost World of the Aegean.* New York: Time-Life, 1976, p. 78.
11. William R. Biers. *The Archaeology of Greece.* Ithaca, NY: Cornell University Press, 1996, pp. 44–45.
12. Arthur Evans. "Knossos: The Palace." *Annual of the British School at Athens.* Vol. 6, 1899–1900, pp. 47–48.
13. Biers. *The Archaeology of Greece*, p. 66.
14. Spivey. *Greek Art*, pp. 38–39.

Chapter 2: Monumental Architecture: Temples

15. Chester G. Starr. *The Ancient Greeks.* New York: Oxford University Press, 1981, p. 97.
16. Thucydides. *The Peloponnesian War.* Translated by Rex Warner. New York: Penguin, 2008, p. 41.
17. Quoted in Thucydides. *Peloponnesian War*, pp. 147–149.
18. Quoted in Thucydides. *Peloponnesian War*, p. 148.

19. Lesley Adkins and Roy A. Adkins. *Handbook to Life in Ancient Greece.* New York: Facts On File, 2005, p. 224.
20. David Sacks. *Encyclopedia of the Ancient Greek World.* New York: Facts On File, 1995, pp. 29–30.
21. Quoted in Peter Clayton and Martin Price, eds. *The Seven Wonders of the Ancient World.* New York: Barnes and Noble, 1990, p. 12.
22. Vitruvius. *On Architecture, Vol. 2.* Translated by Frank Granger. Cambridge, MA: Harvard University Press, 2002, p. 289.
23. Quoted in Peter Green. *The Parthenon.* New York: Newsweek Book Division, 1981, p. 155.

Chapter 3: Other Major Architectural Forms

24. A.W. Lawrence. *Greek Architecture.* New Haven, CT: Yale University Press, 1996, p. 158.
25. Vlasis Vlasidis. "Royal Tombs at Vergina." Museums of Macedonia. www .macedonian-heritage.gr/Museums/ Archaeological_and_Byzantine/ Arx_Bas_Tafoi_Berginas.html.
26. Pliny the Elder. *Natural History.* Translated by Geoffrey B. Waywell. Quoted in "The Mausoleum at Halicarnassus," in Clayton and Price. *The Seven Wonders of the Ancient World*, p. 103.
27. Biers. *The Archaeology of Greece*, p. 207.
28. Lawrence. *Greek Architecture*, p. 122.
29. One well-known group of philosophers who regularly met in a stoa— the Stoics—took their name from the word for that building.
30. Biers. *The Archaeology of Greece*, p. 293.

Chapter 4: Beyond Nature: Greek Sculpture

31. Spivey. *Greek Art*, p. 71.
32. Craven. *The Pocket Book of Greek Art*, p. 35.
33. Thomas R. Martin. *Ancient Greece: From Prehistoric to Hellenistic Times.* New Haven, CT: Yale University Press, 2000, p. 122.
34. Craven. *The Pocket Book of Greek Art*, p. 37.
35. From the *Greek Anthology*. Quoted in Pollitt. *The Art of Ancient Greece*, pp. 51-52.
36. Carl Bluemel. *Greek Sculptors at Work.* London: Phaidon, 1969, p. 30.
37. Pausanias. *Guide to Greece.* Vol. 1. Translated by Peter Levi. New York: Penguin, 1971, pp. 69–70.
38. Plutarch. "Life of Pericles." In *The Rise and Fall of Athens: Nine Greek Lives by Plutarch.* Translated by Ian Scott-Kilvert. New York: Penguin, 1984, p. 198.
39. Pausanias. *Guide to Greece.* Vol. 2. Translated by Peter Levi. New York: Penguin, 1971, pp. 226–227, 229.
40. Pomeroy et al. *Ancient Greece*, p. 458.

41. Pomeroy et al. *Ancient Greece*, p. 458.
42. Spivey. *Greek Art*, p. 372.

Chapter 5: The Pioneers of Greek Painting

43. Robert B. Kebric. *Greek People*. Mountain View, CA: Mayfield, 2001, p. 140.
44. Pausanias. *Guide to Greece*. Vol. 1, pp. 469–471.
45. Kebric. *Greek People*, p. 140.
46. Vitruvius. *On Architecture*. Vol. 2, p. 71.
47. Cicero. "De Inventione." *The Orations of Marcus Tullius Cicero*. Translated by C.D. Yonge. London: George Bell and Sons, 1888, pp. 312–313.
48. Lucian. *Zeuxis and Antiochus*. Translated by H.W. Fowler. Internet Sacred Text Archive. www.sacred-texts.com/cla/luc/wl2/wl207.htm.
49. Pliny the Elder, *Natural History: A Selection*. Translated by John H. Healy. New York: Penguin, 1991, pp. 332– 333.
50. Pliny the Elder, *Natural History: A Selection*. Translated by John H. Healy. New York: Penguin, 1991, p. 333.
51. A different theory proposed by some modern scholars suggests that the Alexander Mosaic was based on a painting by another fourth-century-B.C. artist, Philoxenus (fuh-LOKS-en-us) of Eretria, rather than one of Apelles's works.

Chapter 6: Pottery, Metalwork, and Other Crafts

52. Sacks. *Encyclopedia of the Ancient Greek World*, p. 195.
53. Adkins and Adkins. *Handbook to Life in Ancient Greece*, pp. 182–183.
54. Craven. *The Pocket Book of Greek Art*, p. 103.
55. Craven. *The Pocket Book of Greek Art*, pp. 115–116.
56. Craven. *The Pocket Book of Greek Art*, p. 116.

Glossary

acropolis: "The city's high place"; a hill, usually fortified, central to many Greek towns; the term in upper case (Acropolis) refers to the one in Athens.

agora: A Greek marketplace and/or civic center; the term in upper case (Agora) refers to the one in Athens.

architrave: The horizontal beam resting atop a colonnade in a temple or other Greco-Roman building.

aryballos: A small, round, pottery perfume container.

black figure: A pottery style in which the painted figures and scenes are black against a reddish-brown background.

capital: The decorative top piece of a column.

cella: The main room of a Greek temple, usually housing the cult image (statue) of the god to whom the temple was dedicated.

ceramos: Potter's clay.

colonnade: A row of columns.

Corinthian: A Greek architectural (and artistic) style characterized by columns with masonry acanthus leaves in their capitals.

cult: In ancient times, a group of people who worshipped a specific god, similar to a modern religious congregation.

cult image: In ancient times, a statue of a god that stood in a temple dedicated to that deity.

Doric: A Greek architectural (and artistic) style characterized by columns with plain stone slabs in their capitals.

drum: One of several circular stone sections making up a column's shaft.

faience: A kind of glassware made from crushed quartz or sand.

fresco: A painting done on wet plaster.

frieze: A painted and/or sculpted ornamental band running around the perimeter of a building, most often a temple.

Geometric: A Greek artistic style (and period) characterized by pottery painted with geometric shapes.

Gigantomachy: The mythical battle between the Olympian gods and a race of monstrous giants.

hall: In ancient Greece, a building in which groups of people met, for instance, a town hall.

Ionic: A Greek architectural (and artistic) style characterized by slender columns with curved scrolls in their capitals.

karyatid: A pillar shaped like a woman.

korai (singular *kore*): "Young maidens"; often used to describe female statues whose style was popular in Greece's archaic age.

kouroi (singular *kouros*): "Youths"; often used to describe nude male statues whose style was popular in Greece's Archaic Age.

larnax: A box holding a person's cremated remains.

lekythos: A tall, slender pottery container often used to hold funeral offerings.

meander: The key design commonly seen on Greek pottery.

megaron: In Bronze Age Minoan and Mycenaean palaces, a large hall, usually with a central hearth.

metope: A rectangular space, usually containing paintings or sculptures, in a Greek temple's Doric frieze.

oracle: A message thought to come from the gods; or the sacred site where such a message was given; or the priestess who delivered the message.

orchestra: In a Greek theater, the circular stone "dancing" area in which the actors performed.

order: An architectural style, usually identified by the main features of its columns.

pediment: A triangular gable at the top of the front or back of a Greco-Roman temple.

point: A pointed metal tool used by masons and sculptors to alter and carve stone surfaces.

propylon: A large, often ceremonial gateway.

pteron: A row of columns extending all the way around a temple or other Greek building.

red figure: A pottery style in which the painted figures and scenes are reddish-brown against a black background.

scenographia: "Scene-painting"; in ancient Greek painting, the technique of showing perspective, or depth.

sciagraphia: In ancient Greek painting, the technique of shading.

skene: "Scene building"; a structure facing the audience area in a Greek theater, containing prop storage and dressing rooms for the actors.

stepped altar: A huge stone public structure decorated with colonnades and bands of sculptures.

stoa: A roofed public building, usually long with an open colonnade along one side.

terra-cotta: Baked clay.

tholos: A conical "beehive" tomb commonly built to house deceased Bronze Age Mycenaean royalty.

tumulus: A mound of earth placed above a tomb.

volute: The curved stone scroll in the capital of an Ionic column.

For More Information

Books

Lesley Adkins and Roy A. Adkins. *Handbook to Life in Ancient Greece.* New York: Facts On File, 2005. A very well-researched and easy-to-read compilation of general information about ancient Greece written by two archaeologists.

William R. Biers. *The Archaeology of Greece.* Ithaca, NY: Cornell University Press, 1996. A general overview of Greece's historical periods and the major artifacts from those periods discovered in the nineteenth and twentieth centuries.

Carl Bluemel. *Greek Sculptors at Work.* London: Phaidon, 1969. Written in simple language understandable to all, this volume discusses the tools and methods of ancient Greek sculptors and stonemasons.

John Boardman. *Greek Sculpture: The Classical Period, a Handbook.* London: Thames and Hudson, 1985. This information-packed volume is part of a classic series of books by Boardman, one of the leading modern experts on ancient art.

C.M. Bowra. *Classical Greece.* New York: Time-Life, 1977. One of the great classical scholars of the twentieth century wrote the text of this overview of ancient Greek civilization.

Rodney Castleden. *Minoans: Life in Bronze Age Crete.* New York: Routledge, 1993. A very well-researched, clearly written general synopsis of the Minoans, including their art.

J.J. Coulton. *Ancient Greek Architects at Work.* Ithaca, NY: Cornell University Press, 1995. This book was written by an Oxford University scholar and an expert on Greek architecture.

Robert Flaceliere. *Daily Life in Greece at the Time of Pericles.* Translated by Peter Green. London: Phoenix, 2002. In an easy-to-read text, the author covers nearly every aspect of ancient Greek life, including artisans and their work.

Charles Freeman. *The Greek Achievement: The Foundation of the Western World.* New York: Viking, 2003. A well-written overview of ancient Greek civilization, touching on cultural endeavors as well as history.

Peter Green. *The Parthenon.* New York: Newsweek Book Division, 1981. One of the most respected modern classical scholars focuses on the Parthenon

111

while summarizing Athens's golden age. The book is aimed at students and general readers.

Edith Hamilton. *The Greek Way*. New York: Norton, 1993. The late Hamilton, a renowned scholar of ancient Greece, became famous for this appreciation of Greek civilization.

Reynold Higgins. *Minoan and Mycenaean Art*. London: Thames and Hudson, 1997. Well researched and authoritative, this is one of the best sources available on the subject.

H.W. Janson and Anthony F. Janson. *History of Art: The Western Tradition*. Vol. 1. Upper Saddle River, NJ: Prentice-Hall, 2003. A major study of art history and achievement. Contains a great deal about the evolution of architecture, including numerous, high-quality photos of key structures.

Ian Jenkins. *The Parthenon Frieze*. Austin: University of Texas Press, 2002. Students will find this overview of the Parthenon's Ionic frieze useful, and people of all ages will enjoy the numerous stunning photos.

A.W. Lawrence. *Greek Architecture*. Revised by R.A. Tomlinson. New Haven, CT: Yale University Press, 1996. A terrific general overview of Greece's ancient structures, their features, artistic styles, uses, and so on, with numerous photos and diagrams.

Nanno Marinatos. *Art and Religion in Thera: Reconstructing a Bronze Age City*. Athens: D. and I. Mathioulakis, 2001. A well-documented synopsis of Minoan art in the Aegean Islands by a noted expert.

John G. Pedley. *Greek Art and Archaeology*. 5th ed. Upper Saddle River, NJ: Prentice-Hall, 2011. The text of this informative look at ancient Greek art is clear and easy to understand.

J.J. Pollitt. *The Ancient View of Greek Art*. New Haven, CT: Yale University Press, 2009. A study of Greek art as seen through the eyes of the Greeks themselves.

J.J. Pollitt, ed. and trans. *The Art of Ancient Greece: Sources and Documents*. New York: Cambridge University Press, 1990. Pollitt has compiled a collection of primary source quotes from ancient writers about Greek art, including Plutarch, Pausanias, Strabo, and Pliny the Elder.

Sarah B. Pomeroy et al. *Ancient Greece: A Political, Social, and Cultural History*. New York: Oxford University Press, 2007. Pomeroy, one of the leading U.S. classical scholars, delivers a well-organized and detailed summary of ancient Greek civilization. The text is aimed at students, but adults will find it illuminating, too.

Nigel Spivey. *Greek Art*. London: Phaidon, 1997. Spivey tells the history of Greek art, touching on mythology, religion, drama, changes in the Hellenistic period, and the legacy of Greek artistic endeavors.

Mark D. Stansbury-O'Donnell. *Looking at Greek Art*. New York: Cambridge University Press, 2010. A brief but insightful overview of the Greek arts, with emphases on their changing styles, social and political context, and underlying meanings.

Internet Sources

"Athenian Vase Painting: Black- and Red-Figure Techniques," Metropolitan Museum of Art (www.metmuseum.org/toah/hd/vase/hd_vase.htm). At this site, click on the small pictures of pottery vessels to link to detailed descriptions and colorful photos.

"Greek Painting," Essential Humanities (www.essentialhumanities.net/paint2_2.php). Contains many beautiful photos of Greek paintings on vases and other surfaces.

"The Mausoleum of Halicarnassus," Social Studies for Kids (www.socialstudiesforkids.com/articles/worldhistory/mausoleum.htm). A site for students, with information about the stunning Mausoleum as well as links to other ancient wonders.

"The Parthenon," Great Buildings (www.greatbuildings.com/buildings/The_Parthenon.html). One of the best online sites about the Parthenon, with loads of interesting facts, plus diagrams, floor plans, and more.

"Perseus Project," Tufts University Department of the Classics (www.perseus.tufts.edu). A comprehensive online source about ancient Greece, with hundreds of links to all aspects of Greek history, life, culture, and art, supported by numerous photos of artifacts.

"Seven Wonders of the Ancient World," How Stuff Works (http://history.howstuffworks.com/ancient-rome/seven-wonders-of-the-ancient-world.htm). In this site are striking painted reconstructions of the Seven Wonders of the Ancient World, including Phidias's magnificent statue of Zeus at Olympia.

"The Temple of Artemis at Ephesus," Ephesus (www.ephesus.ws/temple-of-artemis.html). Contains a wonderful reconstruction of what the great temple looked like, along with links to other information about that great ancient city.

"The Tombs at Mycenae," People and Places (www.galenfrysinger.com/tombs_mycenae_greece.htm). This site features numerous photos of artworks from Mycenae, including the "beehive" tombs.

Virtual Sculpture Gallery of Greek and Roman Sculpture (http://mandarb.net/virtual_gallery/sculptures.shtml). Click on any of the links provided, including *Kouros*, "Parthenon Metope," and "Athena," to see photos and/or reconstructions of original Greco-Roman sculptures.

Index

Persian Porch (Sparta), *30*

Perspective, 83–84

Phidias (sculptor), 44, 68, 71, 73–74

studio of, *70*

Philip III (Macedonian ruler), 47

Pitsa tablet, *79*

Pliny the Elder
  on Apelles, 89
  on Chersiphron, 33
  on female painters, 90
  on Mausoleum at Halicarnassus, 51
  on statues of athletes, 65
  on Temple of Artemis, 37

Plutarch, 73, 74

Polygnotus (painter), 80–83, 84

Pomeroy, Susan B., 18, 75

Pottery/ceramics
  amphora, *93*
  black-figure bowl, *94*
  of Classical Age, 96–98
  Minoan, 25–26
  pre-classical, 92–95, *94*

Propylaea, 39, 52–53, *53*, 54

Propylons (monumental gateways), 52–53

Protogeometric period (c. 1050–900 B.C.), 78

pottery of, 92–94, *93*

Pterons, 35

Public halls, 57

R

Red-figure style, *81*, 96, 97

Religion/spiritualism, in Minoan art, 18–19

Roman Empire, cultural fusion with Greece, 11, 13

S

Sacks, David, 36, 95

Scenographia (scene painting), 83

Sciagraphia (shading), 84

Sculpture
  of Archaic Age, 62–64, *63*
  of Classical Age, 64–75
  of Hellenistic Age, 75–77
  in Parthenon, 68, 70–74

Shading, 83–84

Sophilos, *94*

Sparta, 31

Spivey, Nigel, 28, 62

Statues, 65

Stoas, 57–58

Stonemasonry, 41–42

T

Telchines (mythical people), 16

Temple of Apollo (Bassae), 52

Temple of Apollo (Delos), 55

Temple of Artemis (Ephesus), 33, 49

Temple of Athena (Delphi), 55

Temple of Athena Nike, 39, 53

Temple of Hera (Samos Island), *34*

Temples
  early, 32–34
  peripteral, 35
  See also Parthenon

Theater of Dionysus, 56, *56*

Picture Credits

About the Author

Historian Don Nardo is best known for his books for young people about the ancient and medieval worlds. These include volumes on the arts of ancient cultures, including Mesopotamian arts and literature, Egyptian sculpture and monuments, Greek temples, Roman amphitheaters, medieval castles, and general histories of sculpture, painting, and architecture through the ages. Nardo lives with his wife, Christine, in Massachusetts.